Bill & Dave's Memos

A Collection of Bill Hewlett &
Dave Packard's Writings

Edited by

Albert Yuen

2DaysOfSummer Books
Palo Alto, California

THIRD EDITION, SPRING 2007

ISBN 978-1-4243-2781-2

10   9   8   7   6   5   4   3   2

Contents

Dedication

*This book is dedicated to
my father, Chen, and to my brother, Alex.*

Alex, my father, and me in my father's lab at
San Jose State University

Acknowledgments

Thank you Bill and Dave.
(Picture courtesy of Agilent Technologies Archives)

I am grateful to Kerei, my wonderful and supportive wife, who allowed me to work on this book and start a company in the midst of raising four boys. Much thanks also goes to Karen Lewis, who was the HP Archivist at the time of my research for this book. Finally, to all of the folks at Alvesta, who joined us for the vision, for the chance to be a part of something bigger than ourselves.....thank you.

Prologue

This collection of memos by Bill Hewlett and Dave Packard has taken a long journey. I started this work more than 10 years ago while working as an engineering manager at Hewlett Packard Laboratories. In 1996, the founders had long sense relinquished the daily control of the corporation to their successors. Having been a long time employee of HP, I noticed that the corporate culture was slowly changing. Even though there was a lot that had been written about HP already, I wanted to find out for myself how Bill and Dave ran the company on a daily basis. So I started to spend my off-hour time at the HP archives, where much of Bill and Dave's original memos and speeches are kept. As I poured through the boxes of memos, I gained a deeper appreciation of the breadth of the management style that came to be known as the HP Way.

My relationship with HP began 17 years earlier in the summer of '79 when I was a summer intern in the months before heading off to U.C. Berkeley. Having grown up in the Silicon Valley, I was thrilled to be a part of the legendary company that I had heard so much about while growing up. Bill and Dave managed to preserve the spirit of the HP Way from the garage to a global operation over the 40+ years that they directly managed the corporation. Most people think that veteran HP people are sentimental about the "good old days." There's definitely some of that, but if you take the time to learn about the HP Way, you will see that it constitutes some very sound management practices that are beyond sentimental emotions of days gone by.

As I write this prologue, much time has passed since that first summer. I left HP in 1999 to start a company at the peak of the telecom and internet bubble.

Alvesta's original six employees (me-far left, Edmond Lau, Dubravko Babíc, Howard Huang, Julia Liu, and Pierre Mertz)

Several other HP employees and like-minded friends set off to create our own legendary company. Bill and Dave would have been proud to see us setting off with just a dream and very little funding, mainly from family and friends. The early days were so much fun that it hardly seemed like work. We had a three year run and our company was acquired at the end of 2002. The whole experience helped me gain a deeper appreciation of what Bill and Dave endured and overcame to create HP.

I have often gone back to read the memos from the HP archives. As the business world focuses more and more on the performance of each financial quarter, I am always encouraged by the long-range wisdom that Bill and Dave provides in their enduring memos. Their writings discuss a variety of topics from managing people, to technology, to doing business globally. Their discussions on foreign competition and the changing political and governmental forces provide a not-often-seen look into their thinking process.

These memos of decades past continue to have enduring relevance. It is my hope that they will prompt you to think more deeply about the responsibility of the manager.

<u>*Chapter 1*</u>

Management by walking around (MBWA)

"... to preserve the concept that the individual in our organization is a person of infinite worth." [1]

Dave Packard

---

[1] "Personnel the Heart of Management", Dave Packard 10/8/59 (Courtesy of Agilent Technologies Archives)

Bill Hewlett wrote to all the managers in the company on May 6th, 1975 (Courtesy of Agilent Technologies Inc. Archives-Karen Lewis). Note: The underlines were part of the original memo.

"Through the years, one of the most characteristic features of this company has been the effectiveness of communications both upwards and downwards within the organization. On one hand, it is absolutely essential that any manager or supervisor be aware of what is happening in his organization, not just at the level that reports directly to him, but at several levels below that. <u>People are his most important asset and he has a direct responsibility for their training, their performance, for their well being.</u> I want to emphasize the importance of each of you getting around within your organization - <u>talk to the people – find out how they view their job – what they feel would make their job more productive and more meaningful</u>. Encourage your managers and supervisors to take the same active interest. It's amazing what sometimes turns up. On the other hand, it is unfortunate but true, that there are always going to be some cases of legitimate dissatisfaction or misunderstanding in any organization – cases where individuals feel that they are blocked by the "system" or have had serious misunderstandings with their supervisors, or variety of other factors. It is exactly for this reason that we have always had the open door policy for anyone in the company. This feature has been most effective through the years in resolving such problems and is an essential element of the HP way. It serves as a continual reminder to managers of their responsibility to their people if for no other reason than the fact that no one likes someone "going over his head." But if in an employee's opinion, such a step ultimately becomes necessary, it must be understood that he has every right to do so. Any effort to prevent such going "up the line" through intimidation or any other means is absolutely contrary to company policy. Any such action will be considered as a serious breach of management responsibility and will be dealt with appropriately. It is important that this is thoroughly understood within your organization."

Bill

Chapter 2

Bill and Dave's Way

"What is the HP Way? I feel that in general it is the policies and actions that flow from the belief that men and women want to do a good job, a creative job, and that if they are provided the proper environment they will do so." [2]

Bill Hewlett

---

[2] "From the President's Desk," HP Magazine August/September issue 1973. (Courtesy of Agilent Technologies Inc. Archives)

From the president's desk [3]

by
Bill R. Hewlett
(August/September Issue of HP Magazine 1973)

It is estimated that by the end of this year 58 percent of the people at HP will have been with the company less than 18 months. Whereas this is an impressive growth figure, it also poses some real problems.

Any group of people who have worked together for some time, any organization of long standing, indeed, any state or national body over a period of time develops a philosophy, a series of traditions, a set of morals. These, in total, are unique and they fully define the organization, setting it aside for better or worse from similar organizations. At HP all of this goes under the general heading of "the HP way." I want to emphasize that the "HP Way" cannot be demonstrated to be unique, and that although based on sound principles, it is not necessarily transplantable to other organizations. But what can be said about it is that it has worked successfully in the past at HP and there is every reason to believe that being a dynamic "way," it will work in the future. If this is true, and if it differs from more conventional practices, then it is important that whatever this "way" is that it be conveyed to, and understood by, this very large body of new HP people.

---

[3] "From the President's Desk," HP Magazine August/September issue 1973. (Courtesy of Agilent Technologies Inc. Archives)

What is the HP way? I feel that in general terms it is the policies and actions that flow from the belief that men and women want to do a good job, a creative job, and that if they are provided the proper environment they will do so. But that's only part of it. Closely coupled with this is the HP tradition of treating each individual with consideration and respect, and recognizing personal achievements. This sounds almost trite, but Dave and I honestly believe in this philosophy and have tried to operate the company along these lines since it first started.

What are some examples of this application of a confidence in and concern for people? One was a very early decision that has had a profound effect on the company. That decision was that we did not want to be a "hire and fire" operation – a company that would seek large contracts, employ a great many people for the duration of the contract, and at its completion let these people go. Now, there is nothing that is fundamentally wrong with this method of operation – much work can only be performed using this technique – it's just that Dave and I did not want to operate in this mode. This one early decision greatly limited our freedom of choice and was one of the factors that led us into the business in which we are now engaged.

There are a number of corollaries to this policy. One is that employees should be in a position to benefit directly from the success of the organization. This led to the early introduction of a profit-sharing plan, and eventually to the employee stock purchase plan. A second corollary was that if an employee was worried about pressing problems at home, he could not be expected to concentrate fully on his job. This and the fact that in the early days Dave and I were very closely associated with people throughout the company and thus had a chance to see firsthand the devastating effect of domestic tragedy, led, amongst other things, to the very early introduction of medical insurance for catastrophic illness.

As the company grew and it became evident that we had to develop new levels of management, we applied our own concept of management-by-objective. When stripped down to its barest fundamentals, management-by-objectives says that a manager, a supervisor, a foreman given the proper support and guidance (that is, the objectives), is probably better able to make decisions about the problems he is directly concerned with than some executive way up the line – no matter how smart or able that executive may be. This system places great responsibility on the individual concerned, but it also makes his work more interesting and more challenging. It makes him feel that he is really part of the company, and that he can have a direct effect on its performance.

Another illustration of the HP way occurred in 1970. During that time, orders were coming in at a rate less than our production capability. We were faced with the prospect of a 10 percent layoff – something we had never done. Rather than a layoff, we tried a different tack. We went to a schedule with a corresponding 10 percent cut in pay for all employees involved in this schedule. At the end of a six-month period, orders and employment were once again in balance and the company returned to a full workweek. The net result of this program was that effectively all shared the burden of the recession, good people were not turned out on a very tough job market, and, I might observe, the company benefited by having in place a highly qualified work force when business improved.

The dignity and worth of the individual is a very important part of the HP way. With this in mind, many years ago we did away with time clocks, and more recently we introduced the flexible work hours program. Flexible, or gliding, time was originated within the company at our plant in Germany. Later it was tried for six months or so at the Medical Electronics Division in Walham, and then this year made available throughout much of the company. Again, this is meant to be an expression of trust and confidence in HP people as well as providing them with an opportunity to adjust their work schedules to their personal lives.

Many new HP people as well as visitors often note and comment to us about another HP way – that is, our informality and our being on a first name basis. Both Dave and I believe we all operate more effectively and comfortably in a truly informal and personal name atmosphere. Hopefully, with increasing growth we can retain this "family" way of operating with the minimum of controls and the maximum of a friendly, "help each other," attitude.

I could cite other examples, but the problem is that none by themselves really catch the essence of what the HP way is all about. You can't describe it in numbers and statistics. In the last analysis it is a spirit, a point of view. It is a feeling that everyone is a part of a team, and that team is HP. As I said at the beginning, it is an idea that is based on the individual. It exists because people have seen that it works, and they believe in it and support it. I believe that this feeling makes HP what it is, and that it is worth perpetuating.

<u>*Chapter 3*</u>

Why Are We Here?

"I think many people assume, wrongly, that a company exists simply to make money." [4]

Dave Packard

---

[4] "Supervisory Development Program," by Dave Packard, 3/8/60. (Courtesy of Agilent Technologies Inc. Archives)

Supervisory Development Program [5]
Hewlett-Packard Company

(Following is a transcript of the talk given by **Dave Packard**, President of Hewlett-Packard Company, to the training group on March 8th, 1960)

I'm glad to have this opportunity to get together with you and discuss how each of us can do our job more efficiently because as the company grows I think this is going to become crucial in determining whether we are able to continue to grow and keep an efficient organization and maintain the character of our company which we think is important. I am going to speak about things in general, hopefully to give you an idea of our overall objectives. I'm not going into much detail because I am sure others will do that.

I want to discuss <u>why</u> a company exists in the first place. In other words, why are we here? I think many people assume, wrongly, that a company exists simply to make money. While this is an important result of a company's existence, we have to go deeper and find the real reasons for our being. As we investigate this, we inevitably come to the conclusion that a group of people get together and exist as an institution that we call a company so they are able to accomplish something collectively, which they could not accomplish separately. They

---

[5] "Supervisory Development Program", Dave Package, 3/8/60. (Courtesy of Agilent Technologies Inc. Archives)

are able to do something worthwhile – they make a contribution to society (a phrase which sounds trite but is fundamental). In the last few years more and more business people have begun to recognize this, have stated it and finally realized this is their true objective. You can look around and still see people who are interested in money and nothing else, but the underlying drives come largely from a desire to do something else – to make a product – to give a service – generally to do something which is of value.

So with that in mind let us discuss why the Hewlett-Packard Company exists. I think it is obvious that we started this company because Bill and I, and some of those working with us in the early days, felt that we were able to design and make instruments, which were not as yet available. I believe that our company has grown over the years for that very reason. Working together we have been able to provide for the technical people, our customers, things which are better than they were able to get anywhere else. The real reason for our existence is that we provide something, which is unique. Our particular area of contribution is to design, develop and manufacture electronic measuring instruments. The contributions that any group of people makes are, in a sense, the summation of the best efforts of the individuals of that company and a summation of the individual products as well. So our contribution is really measured by the instruments each of you has helped to make – the new instruments engineering has designed to help people make measurements more efficiently, more accurately, more conveniently, less expensively, than they could have done otherwise. So in the last analysis, the reason for our existence and the measure of our success is how well we are able to make our product.

It might be interesting for you to hear a bit about how well we have accomplished this, what our position is in the total field. Many of you are familiar with the summary we made of our 1960 Sonoma Meeting in which we made some studies and estimates as to what part of the total market in various areas is covered by Hewlett-Packard Company's products. We broke this down into numerous instrument classifications and in the case of several instruments, such as signal generators and counters, we supply a very large part of the total number of these kinds of instruments which are used in this country. In the case of vacuum tube voltmeters and audio oscillators, this is true also. We have not supplied as large a portion of industry with some of our other instruments, which have not been in the field as long a time or where we have not done relatively as good a job as our competitors.

I think it is interesting to note that as a result of these studies we concluded that, in the areas where we are making instruments, we are supplying about 1/3 of the country's total requirements. If you include the areas in which we are not competing, but could, we are still supplying about 1/6 of the country's total requirements. This then is a measure of how well our people have met the objectives. But it also indicates that we have a responsibility, in that we are making a very major contribution to the total technical effort of this country. Your efforts are not only worthwhile but you are doing something, which is really significant in terms of total technical effort. You have seen photographs of important scientific work being done – and those photos include –hp- instruments. Those of you who visit the labs of our customers find our instruments are being used in very important work; the advancement of science, defense of our country and many other areas. So – don't overlook our responsibility.

Now, how does the individual person fit into this picture? We have looked at the company and found it exists to make a contribution – not just to make money. I think we can say the same about the people in the company. The individual works, partly to make money, of course, but we should also realize that the individual who is doing a worthwhile job is working because he <u>feels</u> he is accomplishing something worthwhile. You know that those people you work with that are working only for money are not making any real contribution. I want to emphasize then that people work to make a contribution and they do this best when they have a real objective when they know what they are trying to achieve and are able to use their own capabilities to the greatest extent. This is a basic philosophy, which we have discussed before – Management by Objectives as compared to Management by Control.

In other words when we discuss supervision and management we are not talking about military type organization where the man at the top issues an order and it is passed on down the line until the man at the bottom does as he is told without question (or reason). This is precisely the type of organization we do not want. We feel our objectives can best be achieved by people who understand what they are trying to do and can utilize their own capabilities to do them. I have noticed when we promote from a routine job to a supervisory position, there is a tremendous likelihood that these people will get carried away by the authority. They figure that all they have to do now is tell everyone else what to do and quite often this attitude causes trouble. We must realize that supervision is not a job of giving orders; it is a job of providing the opportunity for people to use their capabilities efficiently and effectively. I don't mean you are not to give orders. I mean that what you are trying to get is something else. One of the underlying requirements of this sort of approach is that we do understand a little more specifically what the objectives of the company are. These then have to be translated into objectives of the departments and groups and so on down.

Let us be more specific about the objectives of the company. The first objective is to continue in the field of electronic instruments. We don't plan to go into other areas, at least in the foreseeable future. These instruments are very important in production test applications where people are producing things and need instruments to measure the quality of their product. Similarly in the field of maintenance as the end product goes out in the field, these instruments are needed to make sure the equipment works after it is delivered. So our instruments are used in three general areas; R&D, Production and Field Maintenance. This is a characteristic of most of our

instruments and we have tried to design general-purpose
instruments in most cases. Some of our instruments, however,
are useful only for a specific purpose and in a specific area.

The other objective, which is complementary to this and equally
important, is to try to make everything we do worthwhile. We
want to do our best when we take on a job. We don't intend to
develop a broad line of instruments just for the sake of having a
broad line – we want to design and develop, manufacture and
sell better instruments. The logical result of this is that as we
concentrate our efforts on these areas and are able to find better
ways to do the job, we will logically; develop a better line of
general purpose measuring instruments.

There are important elements at every step of this procedure
and these are really more important than the breadth of the line
or the total market. These are the details of the particular job
involved. In engineering, there are two basic criteria that are
uppermost in the definition of what we hope to be able to do.
As we develop these new instruments, we hope they will be
creative in their design, and they will provide better ways of
doing a job. There are many examples of this – the instruments
our engineers have developed this last year give us some good
examples. The clip-on milli-ammeter, the new wave analyzer,
the sampling scope – all are really creative designs. They give
people who buy them methods of making measurements they
could not make before those instruments were available.

However, creative design alone is not enough and never will be. In order to make these into useful devices, there must be a meticulous attention to detail. The engineers understand this. They get an instrument to the place where it is about ready to go and the job is about <u>half</u> done. The same thing applies in the manufacturing end of the program. We need to produce efficiently in order to achieve our slogan of inexpensive quality. Cost is a very important part of the objective in manufacturing, but producing an instrument in the quickest manner is not satisfactory unless at the same time every detail is right. Attention to detail is as important in manufacturing as it is in engineering. You know, if we send out an instrument with a couple of loose parts, it doesn't make a very good impression on the customer. He loses confidence in our organization. There is no excuse for that kind of performance – either at the top, in the middle or at the bottom. As you move on into supervisory responsibilities, it is your job to see that each person understands what is required and then does his job meticulously.

Selling can be analyzed the same way. We are anxious to find new approaches to selling, but again – detail is important. We certainly are not anxious to sell a customer something he does not want, nor need. You may laugh, but this has happened – in other companies of course, not ours! Also, we want to be sure that when the instrument is delivered, it performs the function the customer wanted.

Financial responsibility is equally important, however different in nature. It is essentially a service function to see we generate the resources, which make it possible for us all to do our job.

These things translated mean that in addition to having the objective of trying to make a contribution to our customers, we must consider our responsibilities in a broader sense. If our main thought is to make money, we won't care about these details. If we don't care about the details, we won't make much money. They go hand and hand.

Now Bill and I feel that our company has a responsibility to our employees. We are not interested only in making a better product. We feel that in asking you people to work for us, we in turn have an obligation. This is an important point and one, which we ask each of you to relay to all the employees. Our first obligation, which is self-evident from my previous remarks, is to let people <u>know</u> they are doing something worthwhile. We must provide a means of letting our employees know they have done a good job. You as supervisors must convey this to your groups. Don't just give orders. Provide opportunity for your people to do something important. Encourage them.

Over the years we have developed the policy that it is important for the supervisor to thoroughly know and understand the work of his group. A debate on this has been carried on by management people for years. Some say you can be a good manager without having the slightest idea of what you are trying to manage, that the techniques of management are all important. There are many organizations, which work that way. I don't argue that the job can't be done that way but I do argue strongly that the best job can be done when the manager or supervisor has a real and genuine understanding of his group's work. I don't see how a person can even understand what proper standards are and what performance is required unless he does understand in some detail the very specific nature of the work he is trying to supervise. We have held closely to this philosophy and we intend to continue to do so. We expect you who are supervising to learn techniques of supervision and keep up to date. I want to emphasize you can supervise best when you know a great deal about the work you are supervising and when you know the techniques of supervision as well.

I want to touch on some other aspects of your work, which are important. As supervisors you will be expected to set high standards of behavior. This is obvious and shouldn't even need to be mentioned. But the example you set is important and I am going to mention specific things, which should be kept in mind. Tolerance is tremendously significant. Unless you are tolerant of people under you, you really can't do a good job of being a supervisor. You must have understanding – understanding of the little things that affect people. You must have a sense of fairness, and you must know what it is reasonable to expect of your people. You must have a good set of standards for your group but you must maintain these standards with fairness and understanding.

We have always considered that we have a responsibility to our employees to plan our work so we can assure job continuity. We do not intend to have a "Hire 'em and fire 'em" operation. This poses some serious considerations.   One is always compelled to find the most efficient way to get a job done. At times it seems the most efficient way is to hire a group of people, work them as hard as possible, and when the job is finished, send them home.   Well, even if this is the most efficient way, we have never operated in this manner. Bill and I do not feel this is the best way for a company like ours to operate.   We have very rigid requirements of technical competence to maintain and rigid requirements in the quality of our equipment. This requires that we have and keep good people at all times. So we feel it is our responsibility to provide opportunity and job security to the best of our ability. This means specifically, sometimes we ask people to work overtime in order to meet customers' demands rather than hire additional people. While this is an imposition in a sense to our employees, it seems to be generally acceptable and we feel it is preferable to "hiring and firing." This is something you all need to understand as supervisors.

Whenever we discuss overall company objectives, we touch on our responsibility to the community at large.   Those things which the institutions in our community provide, the general sense of moral values, the general character of the people that come from the schools, the churches and other institutions; these are things which we accept and are extremely important in the operation of an organization like this. We tend to accept these without second thought. If we consider these matters more seriously, we realize that if these things did not exist, it would have a serious effect on our ability to do a job. So it follows that we do have a responsibility as a company, and as individuals, to help support these activities. You all know that Hewlett-Packard contributes as a company to many of these institutions and we encourage our people to take part – without defining who show do what – but leaving this to free choice.

Last of all, I want to say that I have mentioned our primary objectives but none of these can be accomplished unless the company makes a profit. Profit is the measure of our contribution to our customers – it is the measure of what our customers are willing to pay us over and above the actual cost of an instrument. Only to the extent that we can do something worthwhile, can provide more for the customer, will he year in and year out pay us enough so we have something left over. So profit is the measure of how well we work together. It is really the final measure because, if we cannot do these things so the customer will pay us, our work is futile.

In addition, the margin we have – what is left over after paying for the material, labor, overhead and so on – is the source of our capital for growth. New buildings and facilities and better equipment generally strengthen our position to do a better job.

Our objectives are tremendously vital and, it is your job to help us translate them to all of our employees.

Chapter 4

Our People

"Obviously, we were very close to our employees. We understood their jobs and shared much of their lives with them." [6]

Bill Hewlett

---

[6] "The Human Side of Management," by Bill Hewlett, 3/25/82. (Courtesy of Agilent Technologies Inc. Archives)

The Human Side of Management [7]

Eugene B. Clark Executive Lecture
by
William R. Hewlett
Chairman, Executive Committee
Hewlett-Packard Company

University of Notre Dame
March 25, 1982

I feel most pleased and honored to have been invited to give the third address of the Eugene B. Clark Executive Lecture Series; particularly honored when I consider the two previous speakers - J. Irwin Miller, former chairman of the board of Cummins Diesel, a man with broad background and experience; and Thomas A. Murphy, retired chairman of General Motors.

Irwin Miller spoke on the "uses of freedom". He pointed out that institutions were neither good nor bad but neutral, for it is the people behind institutions -- be it business, labor, government or education -- who form the character of the institution. He then discussed the unique qualities of the American democratic system with its guaranteed package of freedoms, which provide a framework on which a democratic system may operate. However, such freedoms can either be used for good or may be abused.

---

[7] "The Humanside of Management," by Bill Hewlett, 3/25/82. (Courtesy of Agilent Technologies Inc. Archives)

In his "Reflections of a Retired Businessman," Thomas Murphy was stimulated by a conference held at Notre Dame University on the subject of "Can a businessman be a Christian?" His answer was an emphatic "yes". He pointed out that, although most of us start with a certain moral and religious upbringing, we are not always able to have our choice of a career. Murphy's first choice was to be a sports coach, his second a priest; but circumstances directed him into business.

> *"It is important to remember that both Dave and I were products of the Great Depression."*

Nonetheless, you carry these personal beliefs into whatever endeavor you ultimately select. This is the same point Miller made from the other side: Man makes the institutions, not the institutions the man. He went on to discuss business as a tool for social good. He pointed out that the role of management requires the exercise of tough decisions that affect the lives of many people. Temptation is often great to bend the rules, but management must stand strong in its convictions.

In continuing the themes of these two previous speakers I would like to address the subject of "The Human Side of Management". I don't want to approach it as though it were a case study, but I would like to draw on almost 43 years of direct shared-management responsibility in a company that Dave Packard and I founded in 1939 -- a period that saw the company grow from just two people to one that now employs about 65,000 people. I particularly want to talk about the importance we placed on the individual from the very beginning. In no way do I want to suggest that we have "all the answers" or that "this is the only way to do it". But sometimes it helps to go from the abstract to the concrete, and so with this in mind, let me tell you a little bit about the development of Hewlett-Packard Company.

As I talk about the start of the company, it is important to remember that both Dave and I were products of the Great Depression. We had observed its effects on all sides, and it could not help but influence our decisions on how a company should be run. Two thoughts were clear from the start. First, we did not want to run a hire-and-fire operation, but rather a company built on a loyal and dedicated work force. Further, we felt that this work force should be able to share to some extent in the progress of the company. Second, we wished to operate, as much as possible, on a pay-as-you-go basis, that our growth be financed by our earnings and not by debt.

". . . and we did not want to run a hire-and-fire operation . . ."

In the early days, Dave and I tackled almost every job - from sweeping the floors, to keeping the books, to inventing products, and to taking care of the general management of the company. We were very small and insignificant, and we had to employ whomever we could. We had to train them and then hope that they would work out. Reflecting our belief that employees should share in the progress of the company, we initiated a production bonus plan which, in essence, said that we would pay about 30 percent of sales to the employees through a combination of wages and salaries and a bonus thereon. The same percentage was paid to the janitor as to the top manager. This program was immensely successful as there was a quick and direct correlation between output and pay.

Obviously, we were very close to our employees. We understood their jobs and shared much of their lives with them. One of the most difficult steps that I can remember occurred a few years after we had started the company. This was when we had to release our production manager. We finally had to face the fact that, despite everything we had done to improve his management skills, he was not doing

> " . . . *we initiated a production bonus plan . . . the same*
> *percentage was paid to the janitor as to the top manager.*"

the job that needed to be done. Although he was a good friend, it simply came down to a question of his job or the jobs of all the other employees. The impact of that decision is still with us, and in subsequent years has led us to make every effort to find an appropriate niche for a loyal employee. Interestingly enough, we have had good success through the years in relocating such employees within the company.

Another early experience, again related to our close association with our people, was the case of an employee who came down with tuberculosis and was required to take a leave of absence for two years. Here we had the opportunity to observe the devastating impact that it had on his family, and although we were able to provide some help, we determined that this was a problem that we must solve on a permanent basis. Consequently, we established a plan for catastrophic medical insurance to protect our employees from exactly this kind of problem. In the late 1940s this type of coverage was virtually unknown.

During the early years of the company we really had to work with the people on hand. We had to sort out employees according to their abilities, and not by their educational or training backgrounds. Many of those people, who came to us in the early years, are still with us; and a number of them occupy key positions despite the fact they never went to college. Conversely, many of these early employees were not able to live up to the opportunities that were presented to them, and they were forced to recognize that there were limits to their future progress in the company. We worked hard to deal with this problem and, almost without exception, were able to find appropriate jobs for them within the organization. Fellow employees recognized those who were performing well and those who did not measure up. They appreciated that we were trying to find the right niche for each one -- thus preserving our work force.

The type of close relationship that existed in the company encouraged a form of participatory management that has carried on to this day. We were all working on the same problems. We solicited and used ideas from wherever we could get them. The net result was that all felt they were members of the team.

Contrary to most companies at that time, we did not have a personnel department. We had strong convictions that one of a manager's most important jobs was to deal directly with his employees. We did not want to impose any artificial barriers to hinder direct communication.

The informal structure of the company led to what was eventually known as the "open door" policy. In a sense this said that any employee who was unhappy could come in and talk with Dave or me or any other senior executive about his problems. Although such a technique could easily be abused, it never was, and it served as an excellent safety valve for the frustrations that occur in any organization.

A real turning point for the company occurred in 1957, resulting in changes that would have a profound effect on the company in future years. Up to that time, HP was directed by the owner-founders operating in a single plant in Palo Alto, California. Most of the basic policies that directed the company were firmly in place, and we had a good team of people running the operation.

But there were signs of strain appearing. I think the principal concern Dave and I had was that, as it increased in size, the company might lose the intimacy we felt was so important to the organization. Therefore, in January 1957, Dave and I took the top 10 or 12 people of the organization on a weekend retreat to discuss the future of the company, and to decide what action might be taken to insure its continued success.

Several conclusions were reached. First, we decided to divisionalize the company along product lines. We felt that by reducing the size of the operating units and decreasing the span of control, we would provide an opportunity to recapture the personal touch that everyone felt was so important. The managers of these divisions would assume direct responsibility for the health and welfare of their charge, but they would need some guidance. Second, it seemed that this guidance could best be achieved with a simple set of policy statements. In fact, these statements consisted of no more than a codification of past company policies. Coupled with this belief was the conviction that, with these guidelines, local managers could make better decisions than either Dave or me, because -- if for no other reason -- they would be closer to the problems.

Let me summarize these policy statements: The first objective related to profit and set a specific target. It went on to say that all the other things we wished to achieve rested on the success of this first objective.

"The recipe was simple: 1) Have objectives; 2) explain and teach them; 3) gain agreement, with modification if necessary; 4) have everyone share in the success of achievement; and 5) be egalitarian to assure that communications are open".

The second objective dealt with and defined our product line; we should concentrate on the things we know and do best. This was designed to keep us from dissipating our limited resources on business ventures to which we brought no particular knowledge or ability.

The third objective related to our customers, and stressed "inexpensive quality".

The fourth I will read: "To provide employment opportunities for HP people that include the opportunity to share in the company's success which they make possible; further to provide for their job security based on their performance; and to provide the opportunity for personal satisfaction that comes from a sense of accomplishment in their work". This objective goes on to state that "the opportunity to share in the success of the company is evidenced by our generally above average wage and salary level, through the operation of our incentive plan, our recent retirement program and other employee benefits with which you are familiar.

"The objective of job security is shown in a number of ways. Hewlett-Packard has attempted to avoid large ups and downs in its production program because these large ups and downs would require that we hire people for a short period of time and lay them off when we do not need them. It is evidenced by the fact that we have attempted to be lenient with some of our older employees who, as we have grown, have not measured up to the standards we might have reason to expect. But in the interest of those employees who are carrying their full load and who are growing with the company, we have not felt committed to accept anything like an absolute tenure status. Nor do we feel that this policy implies that we must recognize seniority except in cases where other factors are reasonably favorable."

The fifth objective dealt with meeting the obligations of good citizenship, while the sixth spelled out our policy on growth.

These objectives are somewhat similar to the U.S. Constitution - a document expressing basic ideals subject to current interpretation and to amendment. If you look at our objectives as they exist today, you would see how little they have changed despite a hundred-fold increase in sales and a 50-fold growth in employment - and instead of a single plant operation, a company operating with over 50 management units in about 32 countries around the world.

"We have not been afraid to experiment with new ideas, particularly where they might fulfill a desire of our employees . . . "

The recommendations of our 1957 meeting were quickly implemented by divisionalization and by wide distribution of the objectives. These objectives had an important role in training and guiding the new management teams. They served to reinforce the principles of cooperative management -- the concept of leading, not directing. They stressed a management style that was informal, with give and take discussion, lack of private offices, casual dress and the universal use of first names.

But these were not the only changes that took place at Hewlett-Packard that year. For one, the company changed from a privately held corporation to one that was publicly traded. With our stock now on the market, we were able to reward many of our employees with stock bonuses. These bonuses went to a wide variety of officers and employees who had played important roles in the company's past performance.

We concluded the time had come to have a corporate personnel department with a clearly stated role: To support the management team. In no way was it to supplant the direct manager/employee relationship, which we considered so important. In the next three years, basic changes continued to occur. 1958 saw expansion into the European market with sales headquarters in Geneva, Switzerland. To expand our product line we made the first of several acquisitions. A stock option plan was instituted not just for the top few managers,

"You simply cannot run an operation and assume that everything is perfect."

but with the thought that a broad distribution of relatively small options (100 shares) could have real value as a formal indication of a job well done.

The pace continued in 1959 with the establishment of a second manufacturing facility, not in the U.S., as might be expected, but in West Germany. We made a second acquisition, also in the instrument field. We established an employee stock purchase plan with a 25 percent subsidy from the company. This plan, an early forerunner of the Kelso plan, was put into effect with the specific concept that employee stock ownership should give the employee a greater sense of being "part of the company".

1960 saw the establishment of a manufacturing site in Loveland, Colorado. With a multi-plant operation now in place, the former production-bonus system was no longer workable, so a cash profit-sharing plan was established. A key question was: Should the bonus be based on individual plant performance, or should the benefits be spread uniformly throughout the corporation? The answer was easy - it must be corporate wide. Otherwise, the seeds of discord could have been sown among the divisions at a time when it was absolutely essential to pull the teams together.

Thus, in four years since the establishment of a divisional organization with the concept of management by objective, the company had made considerable progress. From an operation in a single plant and a unified management structure with sale of about $20 million and about 1,200 employees, it had grown to a complex organization, with 10 divisions operating in four locations inside the U.S., and two outside the U.S., and with employees and sales each increased by approximately two-and-a-half to one.

The new management structure had been tested by acquisitions, by geographic distribution of plants in both the U.S. and abroad, and by growing size and complexity of organization. The answer was clear: It did work. The recipe was simple: 1) Have objectives; 2) explain and teach them; 3) gain agreement, with modification if necessary; 4) have everyone share in the success of achievement; and 5) be egalitarian to assure that communications are open.

" . . . the people at the top of an organization may have the best intentions in the world of how they want the organization to be run. But there are a lot of layers between the top and the bottom . . ."

Even in a place like Germany, with very different traditions and background, once understood the system worked well. We experienced greater problems with some of the older companies we had acquired in the U.S., particularly where they had operated under a more autocratic rule. Freedom suddenly granted is often hard to cope with (note the problems resulting from the deregulation of a number of U.S. industries). But in the long run it did work.

I will not burden you with a blow-by-blow discussion of the following years. Suffice to say, we greatly reduced our expansion via the acquisition route and turned more to internally generated concepts. By far, the most important of our expansions was in the computation area, first in the scientific and technical fields but, more recently, in general applications.

During the intervening years we continued to give a high priority to the development and welfare of our people. We have not been afraid to experiment with new ideas, particularly where they might fulfill a desire of our employees and have no adverse effect on the company.

Doing away with the time clock was one such step. Flextime - a plan started in our German plant -- is now almost uniformly adopted throughout the company. Under this plan, there is a window for starting work of about two hours, say 6:30 AM to 8:30 AM. Then you simply put in your eight hours and go home. It has been a great success - the employees love it and I am convinced that we get better productivity from our people because of it. Further, it is self-policing, for cheaters are not looked upon with favor by their fellow workers.

One idea that did not prove out was a four-day, 10-hour-per-day plan. We tried it and it simply was not successful. We also made a very bad mistake in trying to make a change in the method of paying employees, one that provided only marginal benefits to the company but greatly inconvenienced our employees. More recently, we adopted a plan to combine vacation and sick leave into a single package that greatly simplifies the complex problem of sick leave accrual and should do much to solve this difficult problem.

One of the most dramatic examples of working with our employees occurred during a recession in early 1970. It became evident that we had about 10 percent more employees than we needed for the production schedule. Rather than lay off or furlough 10 percent of the work force, we simply decided that everyone in the company would take every other Friday off without pay. It worked very well. Employee after employee commented how much they appreciated the opportunity for continued employment, albeit at a reduced pay rate, when on all sides they saw people who were out of a job. After about six months, we were able to return to a full schedule. We helped our people and we preserved our work force, which was essential for continued development.

There are a great many other ways by which we try to take our employees' wishes into consideration. One is to pay heed to the area of the country in which an employee would like to work. This cannot always be achieved but, by and large, much can be done.

Many companies have a policy saying that once an employee leaves you, he will not be eligible for re-employment. We have had a number of people leave us because opportunities seemed greater elsewhere. We take the view that as long as they have not worked for a direct competitor, and if they have a good work record, they are welcome back. They know the company, need no retraining, and usually are much happier for having had an additional work experience. One of our senior executives falls into this category.

The examples I cite are things that employees remember. They comment that "management cares about us" and "we really like it here". This is infectious, because new employees sometimes come to us after a bad work experience elsewhere and start complaining about things at HP (there are always problems). But the veteran employees quickly explain the system, and in short order they become convinced that what we are trying to do is not just talk; it is fact.

But regardless of how hard you try, and how conscientious your people are, the message does not always get through to the rank and file. Certainly, the "open door" policy is a method of taking care of some of the most aggravated problems. It is a safety valve. What you would like, however, is a little more sensitive feedback. You simply cannot run an operation and assume that everything is perfect. There are many ways to achieve this feedback.

"Productivity is the name of the game, and gains in productivity will come only when better understanding and better relationships exist between management and the work force."

One we have tried, and which has been fairly successful, is a technique we call invited. Other employees know in advance who will be attending, and very often they pass on their own questions or complaints.

The format is very simple. After light conversation to break down the barriers, usually an employee will ask a question about something in the company that he does not understand or with which he is unhappy. This provides an opportunity to discuss company policy or company problems.

"We must reinvest in the human side of management."

Sometimes these items are trivial, sometimes the "word" has not gotten down, sometimes the problems are strictly personal and must be treated with great care so as not to interfere with the supervisory process. Sometimes you detect a pattern of problems -- say, for example, inadequate supervisory training. Such problems can be dealt with on a broad company-wide basis. And in any event you always learn more about how the company actually operates. Equally important, employees have a chance to hear first-hand what is happening in the company and what management is trying to do.

A little over two and a half years ago, we tried a somewhat different approach to obtaining feedback on how our U.S. people felt about the company. We employed the services of the International Survey Research Corporation to:

1. Give employees a chance to express opinions about their work place;
2. Provide the company with an opportunity to listen to concerns of the employees and to respond to these concerns and ideas;
3. Compare HP with other large companies with regard to the attitudes of employees; and
4. Set a standard, or benchmark, for future surveys, possibly in other parts of the HP world.

The responses to this survey were very positive. It was clear that the people liked the survey itself as a way of communicating their views. But it was not a one-way program; the survey results were made known to the employees and, where there appeared to be deficiencies, positive remedial actions were taken, and these too were reported. The recommendations for flexible time off came from this source.

One may ask how does all this relate to the human side of management? It relates this way: That the people at the top of an organization may have the best intention in the world of how they want the organization to be run. But there are a lot of layers between the top and the bottom and, in transmitting them from layer to layer, sometimes ideas inadvertently become distorted. It always amazes me at our communications lunches to find out how much some concepts had changed in the transmission process. Feedback such as this is necessary if you wish to determine what is really happening in the organization.

What I have been endeavoring to demonstrate is that there are many creative ways by which an organization can learn the needs of employees and thereby work with them to help them develop a better life style -- a happier work place, a more meaningful existence -- all at practically no added cost to the organization. The old traditional practices must be reexamined to see if they are still valid or necessary. Do they still serve a useful purpose? Or are they just a source of irritation to the employee?

The United States is rapidly discovering that it must be competitive in world markets, and that both cost and quality are factors. Productivity is the name of the game, and gains in productivity will come only when better understanding and better relationships exist between management and the work force.

We must find better solutions to the adversary relationships that have so long dominated the American labor scene. Management is in a position to take the lead in such a new relationship. Managers have traditionally developed the skills in finance, planning, marketing and production techniques. Too often the relations with their people have been assigned a secondary role. This is too important a subject not to receive first-line attention. In this regard we could learn much from the Japanese. We must reinvest in the human side of management.

Personnel – The Heart of Management [8]
Hewlett-Packard Company

(Following is a transcript of the talk given by **Dave Packard**, President of Hewlett-Packard Company, at the Public Personnel Association Conference at the Sheraton-Palace Hotel, San Francisco on October 8th, 1959)

You have been attending conferences this week to discuss and study many of the problems you encounter in your day-to-day work in public personnel administration. Every job of importance always has many problems, so many problems we often become lost in the details and forget what it is we are really trying to achieve. Today, I am going to discuss with you some of the broader aspects of management, for I believe it is of great importance for any manager to have and understand the broad underlying objectives of his job.

In fact, I subscribe strongly to the management approach – which I call "Management by Objective" as opposed to "Management by Control." What I mean is that an organization of well trained intelligent people, working together, can do a job far more efficiently if they understand thoroughly and accept the objectives of the organization and work in an atmosphere of freedom without rigid and extensive direction and control in detail from the TOP. I believe such an

---

[8] "Personnel the Heart of Management", Dave Package, 10/8/59.
(Courtesy of Agilent Technologies Inc. Archives)

organization is basically more efficient than a tightly controlled system of management of the military type where each person is assigned – and expected to do – a specific job, precisely as he is told and without the need to know much or anything about the overall objectives of the organization.

The former is the philosophy of decentralization in management. It is the very essence of free enterprise. It is what causes small business units to be inherently more efficient than large business units, when they are under managers of equal ability in each case. It is essentially the philosophy under which the General Electric Co. has moved in the last twenty years – from a highly centralized organization to complete decentralization with substantial local autonomy for each unit. It is the basic philosophy used by Sylvania and many other large organizations, in an attempt to recapture the efficiency of a small business.

The efficiency of an organization of people working under a common objective in an atmosphere of individual freedom is nothing new. It was demonstrated by Athens against Sparta over twenty centuries ago. There is much evidence – both from history and from current experience to demonstrate that an organization, which can preserve a high degree of freedom for the individual within its ranks – is likely to be the most efficient.

I am aware that there are many special problems in the field of public administration that are not present in private business administration. The safeguards, which are built into our legislative system, result in controls on public administration, which seem frustrating to a person in a private enterprise. Dealing with pressure groups must be a trying experience, at least on occasion. I am aware, therefore, that the possibility of increasing individual freedom in public administration involves many difficulties, some well beyond the control of your group. I am aware too that many people are working for more centralization, for more policies and more details as well, to be decided at the highest level – preferably by Washington. Much of this pressure comes from the erroneous concept that if the Federal Government pays, it doesn't cost the state or you anything…and so on down the line. Much of the incentive for public administration to be centralized in a higher authority comes from the belief that political pressures are important and must be exerted at the highest levels by all groups. Unfortunately many yield to these pressures under the false impression that concentration of administrative power in higher authority will also make administration more efficient.

One cannot dispute the fact that the number of people under public administration is increasing and increasing rapidly in many areas. For those of us who believe that the government – at all levels – should do only those things, which clearly cannot be done by private enterprise – this trend is disturbing.

But regardless of the trends and regardless of our personal feeling about them – the fact is – you people in the field of public administration are doing a very important job. Your job is increasing in importance and we should therefore place great emphasis on how public administration can best be accomplished. I sincerely believe it is possible to apply the philosophy of management by objective to public administration and that a broader application of this principle of individual freedom in management is desirable in your field.

Just a month ago I returned from a short visit to Russia. I had the opportunity to visit a number of factories – which of course are all owned and operated by the government – in that sense under public administration. The recent visit of Khrushchev and the fact that many of our people have visited Russia recently – has caused us all to think more about their system and to try to learn more about it. I would like therefore – to take a minute or two to draw some comparisons between their management techniques and ours.

First, they have moved a long way from the basic philosophy of Communism – if indeed they ever had it. There is no application of the principle expressed as "from each according to his ability – to each according to his need." The people do not own anything – it is all owned by the State.

They have the most highly centralized system imaginable. The government bureaus control everything – they set wages, working hours, rent, prices, work quotas for factories. And – they have found this high degree of uniformity has brought a high degree of inefficiency to the extent they have backed down in the last few years. They have adopted a number of techniques from the capitalist system in order to make their administration more efficient. They recognize that monetary incentives are important. They have established rate ranges for various jobs to encourage and reward performance. These rate ranges establish and recognize status among groups of individuals with the organization – just as definitely as do our own rate ranges. For example – the salaries of schoolteachers are determined by the amount of education the teacher has obtained – by the length of service – and by the grade, which is taught. In California – we have adopted a single salary schedule and we recognize only two of the three factors mentioned – education and length of service. The salary range of teachers in Russia is from 650 to 1500 rubles per month – a range greater than you will find in most California schools.

In a factory – you will find a salary or wage range from 450 rubles to 3500 rubles per month – not including the top management echelon. It would appear that they have as much if not substantially more – flexibility to use base salary as a reward for ability and performance than do we in most cases. I think if you compare these ranges with the salary ranges you have established in your own organizations – you will find their range is substantially greater. Even more important – the top of their range is generally much further above the average than is the case in this country. In other words, they have monetary mechanisms affecting base pay for encouraging outstanding performance among their top-level people.

The administration of a Russian factory has the responsibility of providing nurseries for the children of the working mothers.

Housing, mass apartment housing, for the workers is also his responsibility and he can use this authority to distribute apartments to individuals and thus encourage and reward performance where it will improve the efficiency of his administrative unit.

They also have a system of monetary group performance incentives for most of their organizations. If the factory (under government ownership and equivalent to public administration of course) exceeds its quota – the employees receive a bonus, which may be as much as 100% of base salary and seemed to average at least 30% in most of the bases I encountered. It is as though we had a system whereby if the highway department would exceed the schedule in building new roads – every employee in that department would receive a substantial monetary bonus – paid monthly and in proportion to their superior performance. I suggest you go home and try that on your legislative body!

These group incentive plans seemed to favor the more important industries with higher bonuses. A tractor factory or a factory making generators for the large power stations would be favored with a bonus of from 50% to 100% of base pay whereas in a less important industry, the bonus would ordinarily be about 30%.

They use other techniques to reward individual performance. These include public recognition of the individual as well as monetary rewards. Each factory had a large billboard where pictures of the outstanding workers were shown each month. In the center of each city – they have similar billboards where there are posted pictures of workers who do a job of national importance. The people so honored are those who have received the so-called Lenin Prize which also carries a stipend of 1500 rubles – the average pay for two months.

They have learned from experience that they must recognize individual differences. They now provide these incentives in order to achieve a reasonable degree of efficiency in their administrative units. They have learned too, that the central authority is not always blessed with the greatest wisdom. They are now encouraging managers of smaller units to exercise more authority in setting their quotas and in making other management decisions.

It is the observation of almost everyone who visits Russia that the people there work hard and have a religious devotion to their cause. In other words, a broad well accepted common objective – which is the work for a better life for their government as well as the people.

Yet you see much evidence of great inefficiency. People waiting around for someone else to make a decision. Two people doing the job of one – outdated tools and methods on many jobs. You can measure their performance in terms of prices and in terms of the number of man hours necessary to do a job – and by every measure you can apply – you find the real efficiency of their administration is much lower than ours. Finally, you sense that although they have the most highly organized and most highly centralized and controlled system of management that can be conceived, although they have used nearly every technique in our book – they have failed completely to use the most important of all – that of recognizing the individual as a person important for his own sake.

This now, brings us to the very heart of the problem. What is the real purpose of an organization of people. Is the purpose of the private factory simply to make a profit for its owners – is the only purpose of a highway department to build and maintain highways – the fire department to be the most efficient organization of highly disciplined and highly trained people ready to put out the fire at the sound of the gong? Certainly, one of the proper objectives of management is to develop an organization to do these specific tasks for which it is designated. It is the function of the personnel man to obtain the people – and to assist management in their development, growth and direction – to help in every way in the overall objectives of the organization.

In other words – we can say that an important purpose of an organization is to serve society. But if we stop here – there is no way in the world to detect such an organization in America from an organization in Communist Russia. These organizations are manned with highly trained people. Their managers are capable. They use techniques, which appear to be as good as our best. They are dedicated to serve society – which they call the people.

But there is a difference – a difference so important that is unbelievable we overlook it so often. The difference is that in America – each individual is a person of infinite worth. He is no different during the eight hours a day he is at work in your organization than he is in his home – or in his church. Whether he be Mohammedan, Christian, or Jew – he is an individual worthy of individual blessing from his God. And in America we must always remember he is an individual too in his job. So ladies and gentlemen – as you go home from this conference to put into effect the things you learned here to make your organization more efficient – remember that we are engaged in a struggle to the death with this malignant social disease called Communism. Remind yourself of the nature of the struggle. The struggle is not just capitalism vs. communism as an economic system – it is something far more important – as important as such considerations may be.

The real question is the person vs. the people. Remind yourself that the leaders of Communism have never hesitated to strike down the individual ruthlessly – when he stood in the way of alleged progress of the people. When the Hungarians were so bold as to express themselves, they were ruthlessly shot down. Even the leader who shows signs of deviation – deviation from blind support of the Communist State is either shot or sent to Siberia. Every person knows he is under continual surveillance of the police – watching him to make sure he shows no expression of individuality. As you travel in Russia – you can sense this very strongly. The people are friendly but they are afraid.

Groups of students were eager to ask questions about America but they were afraid to be seen with an American. They would not come and sit in the Hotel lobby – they felt safe only if they were walking.

ENOUGH TIME?

> Story about students and police
> Story about freedom of speech
> Story about telephone and pillows
> Story about visiting apartment

On every side you see evidence that the individual person counts for nothing. It makes little difference if he is run over by an automobile – it makes no difference what he thinks. His only purpose in life is to serve the State and he ceases to exist unless he submits himself completely to domination by the State.

So the real question involved is this – are we, in our management philosophy and in our personnel administration – going to work to preserve the concept that the individual in our organization is a person of infinite worth. That the organization exists to serve the individual as well as to serve society. To the extent you are able to keep this as one of your basic objectives – you will insure for your organization that efficiency which comes only from enthusiastic people using their energy and their imagination in an atmosphere of freedom – working for a common objective. This opportunity exists best in the field of public administration when the responsibility is in the smallest unit possible and looks to the lowest level of local government for control.

This course provides greater incentives for people at all levels, it will attract more capable people to your ranks. Most important of all – you will do much to strengthen the cause of personal freedom throughout the world – if you make sure it is encouraged within your own organization.

This then is the heart of your job in personnel administration – to make sure your management has a heart.

<u>*Chapter 5*</u>

Engineering Management

"I want to emphasize then that people work to make a contribution and they do this best when they have a real objective when they know what they are trying to achieve and are able to use their own capabilities to the greatest extent." [9]

Dave Packard

---

[9] "Supervisory Development Program," by Dave Packard, 3/8/60. (Courtesy of Agilent Technologies Inc. Archives)

Technology and Profitable Growth [10]
By
William R. Hewlett
April 20th, 1977
(Addressing General Electric's Engineering Staff)

Last year, Hewlett-Packard finally arrived at that exalted position of having sales top the $1 billion mark. General Electric was just about that size the year we started our company – 38 years ago – so we are still a little bit behind you.

In a sense, then, my talking with you tonight about technology and profitable growth might seem like carrying coals to Newcastle. However, I have spent my entire professional life dealing with these matters, and I firmly believe that regardless of a company's size some element of its operations can stimulate interest and lead to valuable discussion.

I will try to be fairly practical in my comments – for engineers, as I know them, are very practical people. As a matter of fact, there is a great story about engineers that I think bears this out. It concerns three Frenchmen – a priest, a lawyer, and an engineer. Each had allegedly committed a heinous crime, and they were to be executed by the guillotine. The first to be executed was the priest. He said, "I want to lie on my back so that I can look up at God, and he will understand my

---

[10] "Technology and Profitable Growth" Bill Hewlett, 4/20/77. (Courtesy of Agilent Technologies Inc. Archives)

problems." Since his executioners couldn't see anything wrong with that, he was tied down suitably and they pulled the lever. The knife came down and stopped. For a moment there was a great hush in the crowd, and then they roared, "Oh! an act of God, an act of God. You must let him go!" There was nothing to do but unstrap him and let him up. The lawyer, pleased with these results, said, "I want to be executed lying on my back, too." Once again the knife came down and stopped, and the lawyer cried out, "See, a great injustice has been done, a great injustice has been done!" So they had to let him go, too. The engineer was not to be outdone. He, too, was tied down lying on his back. But just as they were about to release the knife, he yelled out, "Wait a minute, wait a minute! I think I see the problem!"

In the course of thinking about how I might approach my subject for tonight, I was reminded of some of our experiences in the early days of the Hewlett-Packard Company. It was a very small enterprise by any standard of measurement, and because it was, we were pretty much on our own when it came to learning the nuances of business management. Our exposure was very practical and first hand – not something we could learn from textbooks – and out of it all came the gradual development of the policies and practices that have guided the company down through the years.

When we started our company we had very limited facilities, and we had to work with people who just happened to walk through the front door. We learned very quickly that these people were inherently honest, that they wanted to do the right thing, and that given the opportunity, they would do it. We found that by respecting the dignity and worth of these people, there was much they could contribute. I believe that a very great deal of what we subsequently accomplished in the company is a direct result of this very basic approach to people.

Engineering of Opportunity

We also had some learning to do regarding the management of our engineering effort. We were not able to hire the top engineers – we even had to take Packard from GE – so we had to figure out how to use our resources as efficiently as possible. We derived what I called, for lack of a better term, "engineering of opportunity." The idea was that instead of saying to our small engineering staff, "Here is a device we want developed, now go forth and do it," we preferred to search out customer test and measurement problems and then say to our engineers, "What technology can we apply to solve these problems?" By staying within the bounds of our technological capabilities, we were able to invent a large number of useful products for our customers, while at the same time saving ourselves a tremendous amount of effort.

Another learning experience in engineering management occurred in the mid-fifties after the company was quite a bit larger. Someone in the company invented a "vintage chart" on which we plotted the annual sales of products over a period of four or five years. We found that the average life of a product was surprisingly long, and that our entire growth was heavily dependent upon adding layers and layers of new products. This impressed upon us as at a very early stage that the route to growth was through new products – products that contributed real value content to our catalog.

Other Early Lessons

We also learned the hard rule, in the early years of the company, that if you want to do something, you had better earn the dollars first. (Fortunately, in those days, we were not subjected to the siren calls of investment capital.) This philosophy of pay-as-you-go also had a long-term influence on how we approached management problems.

A final, and very key learning experience for us, was discovering the advantage of having a relatively small group of people working together closely – people who knew what they were doing, and where they were going. This was a characteristic we wanted to preserve, and even though our volume was only about $50 million at the time, we believed that the method for doing that was to decentralize. We also recognized, however, that to follow that course we would have to develop an overall operating philosophy to guide our decentralized units.

We chose a concept that is now popularly known as "management by objectives" – although I can assure you we had not heard the name at that time. Basically, our approach was to divide the company into several small operating divisions with well-defined product lines, to assign managers with complete responsibility for all their functional areas, and to provide them with some broad, general guidelines.

Broad Objectives

Then, Dave and I sat down and wrote six corporate objectives. The first of these dealt with the essence of everything we were trying to do – make a profit. The other objectives covered customers, fields of interest, growth, people, and citizenship.

Although we have reviewed and modified these objectives from time to time, they really have not changed very much over the years. We added a seventh objective in the 1960's on management techniques, but this simply reflected the increasing size of the company. These objectives have withstood the test of time, and our ability to follow them so steadfastly has been a major factor in the company's achievements.

Four "Musts"

A few years ago, to try and boil down these objectives into a few catch phrases, I coined what I call the four "musts" at HP. You must make a profit, you must make that profit by technological contribution, you must work through people to achieve these objectives, and you <u>must</u> put back more into the community than you take out. Let me discuss those themes.

It doesn't matter whether you start with technology, or start with profit – one is dependent on the other. For discussion purposes, then, I will begin with technology.

To make a technological contribution you have to have good people, and you have to provide the proper atmosphere. It is obvious, I think, that good people attract good people, thus producing an exciting place to work. This is a positive feedback type of operation, and if you can get into this mode, it is extremely beneficial.

The need for a creative atmosphere requires a little more discussion. It has to do with the psychology or the mentality of engineers. As I know them, engineers are very dedicated, conscientious people, and what they really want is an opportunity to influence directly the course of the company's business. R&D people don't want to be on the sideline; they want to feel that they have a major role in defining what a company does. And, they can play a major role if they are given the opportunity to do so.

At HP, product decisions are almost always made between the divisional manager and the R&D personnel – not, in contrast with many companies, between the divisional manager and the marketing operation. In our business, we feel that – important as they are – marketing people must play a secondary role in the question of production definition.

Being on the Cutting Edge

This is a very important point for R&D engineers. They look at their jobs very differently if they feel they are in on the cutting edge of what the company is going to do, rather than being around to merely carry out pre-determined programs. This, of course, is the basis of one of our objectives – that you must make a technological contribution, not take a "me too" approach. If you had the opportunity to listen in on one of our management sessions, you would find that many approaches are rejected because people feel there is not enough of a technical contribution to justify bringing a particular product to market.

There are a number of benefits in starting from the engineering side up. In the first place, it allows you to re-define a project as you are going along, instead of having to operate under a fixed set of specifications that come from the outside and must be followed very closely. Secondly, it allows the engineering staff to optimize their programs by providing trade-off opportunities. They can say, "If I give a little bit here, I can get an awful lot more there, and probably come up with a much better product as far as the ultimate customer is concerned." Thirdly, you also have the ability to seize ideas of opportunity.

I'm gong to give you several examples, and you can be quite sure that these will be ones that do not occur every time – but they are legitimate.

Some Good Examples

A number of years ago we were getting involved with a lot of digital work, and the primary tool was an oscilloscope. One of the engineers recognized that he really did not care what the wave shape was – all he needed to know was whether the state of a particular node was a zero or a one. He got to thinking that if he had a simple device to attach that would indicate the current state, it would be very helpful. So, he devised a unit with an LED that was either on or off in accordance with the state of the node. He had several of them made and the instrument was so effective that it was decided to put it on the market. Before we had to redesign this product several years later, we had sold $1.5 million worth, and made a good profit. But beyond that, it opened up a whole new area of business for us. When I describe it now it all seems pretty obvious, but it wasn't so obvious when that engineer first started thinking about the problem.

Another example – and it may almost sound as though I am contradicting myself – was our entry, for one reason or another, into the laboratory power supply business. In a sense this is a very unromantic and uninteresting business, and while we were doing fairly well in it, we weren't doing anything outstanding. A number of years ago we put a very good engineer – a hard-nosed Dutchman – in charge of the operation. He was there for a while, and finally came down complaining. He said, "You know, Bill, I don't want to spend all my life making those damn power supplies." The answer was, "John, we've got to have someone run that operation, and you're stuck."

So John went back, called his staff together, and said, "Look, there's got to be a better way of making power supplies. This old routine analog approach is a very inefficient one." After many days of discussion and review, they came to the decision that the switching power supply was the way to go. They needed a special transistor, which they persuaded our central laboratory to develop, and with that John and his people turned their power supply product line into a very viable part of our business, -- one that makes better than average corporate profits. Perhaps the significance of their effort is most readily apparent in the fact that our other operating divisions, on their own, are deciding that they want to use these power supplies in their own equipment and you all know how reluctant one group is to use equipment from another group.

One final example where putting the ball in the engineering court can really pay dividends is the case where just plain business strategy requires that you enter a new product area. As many of you know, we are in the computer business. In this business, as in many other businesses, you want to supply as much value-added equipment as you can. Our problem was that while we were making the mainframe, we had to acquire a large portion of the peripherals from the outside, and we don't really make much money on the non-value-added equipment. One important peripheral was a disc memory, so we set up a group and told them, "We want you to put us in the disc business." They weren't given any specification to follow. We simply said, "Here's the field we want to get into, now you define the particular item you can build." The presumption was that they would design it on the best technology available within the company. That, of course, is exactly what happened.

Engineering Management

This degree of engineering involvement obviously requires people in divisional management who understand engineering. It's not by accident, therefore, that 35 of our 36 or so divisions are headed by people with engineer's degrees. (For those of you who are interested, less than a quarter have an MBA.) This means, of course, that we are basically taking people who have not been trained in management and putting them into key management slots. In turn, this approach requires a strong commitment by top management to provide these divisional people with considerable back-up support.

Certainly a prime responsibility of top management is the allocation of resources. One of the key resources is the percentage of sales that we allocate for research and development. A typical number for us is about 10 percent, and of that approximately 1.5 percent goes to corporate laboratories and the remaining 8.5 percent to the operating divisions. Determining the percentage that each division is going to receive is very important, and we allocate this based on our views of a division's potential in its particular field, the quality of its people, and the medium and long-range goals we are trying to achieve.

One area where we differ from many other companies is our willingness to make the commitments necessary to develop our own key components. Our decision to go this route was made many years ago, right after the end of World War II. At the time, we were designing a high-frequency voltmeter. We had come to the conclusion that a key component was a very special diode, and Eimac agreed to fabricate the diode for us. By designing and incorporating that diode, we were able to build a top-line voltmeter that was very successful in the marketplace. This convinced us that we could afford to invest a considerable amount of money for in-house developments of key components if, indeed, they produced a product that made us more competitive.

Deep Commitment to ICs

Today, for example, we are deeply committed to the development and production of special solid-state devices for our own use. We now have nine divisions with integrated circuit facilities, and a tenth just coming on-stream. People from the semiconductor industry tell us that no one can afford to spread such sizeable capital resources out among nine or ten areas – be we don't look at it that way. Our feeling is that while we won't make money on integrated circuits, per se, we will profit from the sale of products built around those integrated circuits. As an indication of that, I would guess that probably 90 to 95 percent of our products now have one or more of our proprietary integrated circuits in them.

When I asked our people recently how much we are spending on IC production for in-house use, I was told that it is about $30 million at cost. In addition, we've invested about $30 million in capital facilities for this program – so you can see that there has been a major commitment by management to provide our engineering staffs with the resources that will allow them to develop products that are superior to those of our competitors.

A fairly recent example of this commitment was our decision to pursue silicon-on-sapphire semiconductor technology. We knew that a number of important companies had looked at SOS and that they had concluded that it was not a feasible approach. Nonetheless, after considerable research, we believed that this technology was best suited for our computers. We invested between $10 million and $15 million on the project, and our entire computer operation is hinged upon that gamble. I think, as of now, that it was a good gamble because we are beginning to produce these devices, and they are demonstrating the performance that we anticipated.

The SOS decision leads almost directly into the next subject – stress on profits. If you are going to take a gamble on this magnitude (and $15 million is a sizeable one for us) you have to have a certain level of financial security. One measure of financial security is whether you've been able to finance your growth from earnings, or whether you've had to engage heavily in debt financing. As I indicated earlier, at HP we have always had a very strong belief that we needed to concentrate on growth from within. It is for that reason that we have continually stressed the importance of profits to HP people at all levels of the organization.

Profit...A State of Mind

Profit, as far as I am concerned, is a state of mind. It is not something that the boss is harping on; instead, it is something that each person in the organization must be convinced is in his own best interest. Once that attitude prevails, each individual will have a direct concern that his part of the organization is making a profit. I think that concern is even more important for technical people. Because in a more sophisticated sense, profit is the difference between what an item cost you, and what your customers perceive its value to be – that is, the technical contribution if your are in the technical field. I think that every one of our technical people now appreciates this fact fully. They recognize that if you are going to make a profit, it has to be on the basis of some kind of contribution.

Whereas profit is everyone's business, R&D had the opportunity to exert some of the very highest leverage to provide profit. A good idea, properly executed, can generate a tremendous amount of profit. Although I swore to myself that I was not going to talk about them, pocket calculators provide a good example of the very high leverage you can derive from high-risk R&D projects, if they are successful. At one time, pocket calculators represented a significant portion of our total corporate earnings – so it was a very fortunate gamble in that regard. This earnings imbalance did create some problems which have since resolved, but the point remains that an outstanding technical contribution can have a tremendous impact on profitability.

First Hand Experience

I would like to say one final word about profit before going on to the next subject. As I indicated earlier, profit is everyone's concern – and that includes the boss. If the boss concentrates on managing four areas and forgets about three others, those three forgotten areas are very likely going to have an adverse effect on profit performance.

We had first-hand experience with this several years ago when we discovered that we simply were not generating enough profits to cover our expansion rate. We took a very careful look at this and found that rather than being a financial problem, it was a management problem. For one thing, the bosses were just not doing a very good job in managing current assets. For another, they were under-pricing new products in anticipation of high volume at a later date. For the most part, their intentions were good (gain market share, maintain adequate inventories, etc..), but they just didn't see the total picture.

We turned the situation around by putting emphasis on current assets and by raising prices. This accomplished two things: it slowed down our rate of growth, and it certainly brought more money into our coffers. I cite this example merely to reemphasize that the overview top management can provide is particularly important in an engineering-oriented company such as ours.

The third "must" at HP is working through people to achieve objectives. I really don't need to elaborate on this subject, because I think of all the companies I know, GE is the most conscious of this need and has done the best job. I would only add this one comment: management by objectives is an extremely costly program. It requires a very large number of managers because you are spreading the workload among a great many people. Additionally, if you are drawing your management talent from the engineering staff, it is important to recognize that these people have not been trained either in delegating responsibility or in management principles. Therefore, it is essential that you provide training and development programs and facilities to be sure that when you put these people into management positions they are indeed able to handle them.

I will not take the time tonight to comment on the fourth "must" – the general subject of one's responsibility to the community. That is a very broad area with many ramifications. I just want to assure you that we supported the concepts of good citizenship long before it became the popular thing to do.

No Perfect System

Let me sum up what I have been saying. It is obvious, I think, that there is no perfect system for managing a company. Every system creates some new problems. But, as I look back on our experience at HP, I can draw some general conclusions.

We really have not solved the problem of the dual ladder. I know that you people have given this a lot of thought too, and the solution still lies in the future.

In terms of management by objectives, I think we have had reasonably good results at the upper levels. The approach has been quite successful as a motivation for our engineering staffs, for example. But I have some doubts as to the degree to which it operates at the lower levels in the corporation – and that, of course, is one of the places we would like to have it operate more effectively. We intend to work on this problem.

I believe we have been reasonably successful in making profit a viable concept in practically everything we do, and that the profit center itself has been satisfactory despite some shortcomings. We have accomplished this partly by our management-by-objectives approach, and partly by creating a special management accounting system that tends to remind managers where our primary focus should be.

Finally, at HP we have committed ourselves to the concept that achieving profit and growth via a constructive R&D program on a pay-as-you-go basis is the path we want to follow. For us, at least, this approach has proved successful in the past, and I see no reason why it will not continue to work for us just as well in the future.

Chapter 6

Managing for the Future

"These kinds of problems are not surprising in view of the complexity of our company operations, combined with the high rate of growth in 1972 and 1973, but they do not represent the management excellence Bill and I hoped we might have achieved." [11]

Dave Packard

---

[11] "Managing Hewlett Packard for the Future," by Dave Packard, 3/17/75. (Courtesy of Agilent Technologies Inc. Archives)

Managing Hewlett Packard for the Future [12]
Hewlett Packard Executive Seminar
March 17, 1975
By
Dave Packard

I am pleased to welcome you to this seminar you will be attending this week which is a new management development program in our company.

I would like to begin by outlining why this new program was established and what we hope it will accomplish. On this point I have somewhat of an ulterior motive − If I tell you what I hope you will get out of this program it may have some effect on what you try to get out of it.

As you all know, it has been a long-standing policy of our company to provide a wide range of opportunities for all of our people to advance within the company. It is my job and it is the job of each one of you to see that this policy applies to all people on an evenhanded basis, regardless of race, religion or sex.

I believe we have done a fair job in providing opportunities for people to improve themselves and to move ahead in the

---

[12] "Managing Hewlett Packard for the Future," Dave Packard, 3/17/75. (Courtesy of Agilent Technologies Inc. Archives)

company. I am convinced; however, we can and must do a better job.

The real motivating reason for this program was the realization at the end of fiscal 1973 that the company was heading for some serious problems in the financial area and this difficulty was the result of our failure to manage some of the affairs of the company the way they should have been managed.

Our company had experienced a very rapid growth in 1972 and 1973. This was the result of an expansive period in the world economy, during which we had introduced an unusual number of outstanding new products.

In this environment of high demand for our products and a sellers market for material and labor, we failed in at least three areas to do the right kind of a job in managing our affairs.

We allowed our inventories to grow more rapidly than necessary.

We were lax in collecting accounts receivable on the sale of our products at a time when demand was high and when payment discipline could easily be enforced without any impact on volume.

We neglected to keep profitability up at the very time when it should have been at its highest level. Price controls made it difficult to improve profitability on older products, but to a large degree the problem of profitability was our fault because we failed to price new products properly. This was because of a failure on the part of some of our managers to recognize that it is very seldom safe to price a new product on the basis of anticipated high volume production costs before the high volume production costs have in fact been achieved.

By failing to recognize this very important management principle, we built into our pricing on some important new products an assured loss – and it was difficult to correct the situation under price controls.

We had some other problems in the management area in addition to the three main problems I have mentioned. At least one major product was put on the market before it was fully developed. I would like to add parenthetically – this caused some personal chagrin, after preaching for three years in Washington about the evils of putting a new weapon system into production before it has been developed to find that some of my proteges in the management ranks here at HP had made the same fatal mistakes.

And I also found a number of cases where management responsibility had not been clearly defined. I called on one marketing office after I returned from Washington in 1972 and asked who was in charge, and no one in the office knew who was in charge.

These kinks of problems are not surprising in view of the complexity of our company operations, combined with the high rate of growth in 1972 and 1973, but they do not represent the management excellence Bill and I hoped we might have achieved.

This program thus was motivated by some of the management mistakes we made in 1972 and 1973 and we hope it will serve to improve the management of our company, particularly at the middle and upper management levels.

I would say that these management problems, which became visible and serious at the end of 1973, were the result of two management attitudes, which have caused similar problems in many companies.

The first is the failure of management to recognize that it is just as easy to make a profit today, as it will be tomorrow. Actions taken which result in reducing short-term profit in the hope of increasing long-term profit are very seldom successful. Such actions are almost always the result of wishful thinking and almost always fail to achieve an overall optimum performance.

There are two kinds of management actions that can cause great trouble in this area. One, which I have alluded to, is to price a new product on the basis of what one hopes the cost of production will be in the future. The only safe way is to price it on the basis of what you know the cost will be – and if in doubt, add a margin, don't subtract it, and then reduce the price only if, in fact, the cost is reduced.

There is always the rational that if we keep the price down, the volume will build up and this will make it possible to get the cost down.

There is of course something to this line of reasoning, but it is very dangerous. If the pricing does not in fact get the volume up, there is a problem. And if the increased volume, even if it is achieved, does not get the cost down, there is a problem.

If one is lucky, action based on this line of reasoning can be very successful.

Management decisions should not be based on the hope for luck. We must seek in our management decisions those, which will provide a high assurance against failure, and I believe this can be done without reducing the opportunities for success.

And so on this matter of pricing, let's play it safe in the future and price new products in accordance with known costs. We can always bring prices down as costs come down.

Furthermore, if the new product is really as good as it should be, we will sell as many as we can make in the early period of the product life at the higher price.

These cost-pricing problems have been centered primarily at the division level and should not, in my view, be moved up to more corporate involvement. In the final analysis, decision on pricing will have a large influence on the profitability of the individual division, and the division management people making these important pricing decisions must be judged by the profitability of their divisions, which result from their pricing decisions.

<u>The second problem which became more serious in 1973 had to do with the balance between what is best for the division and what is best for the company.</u>

Clearly, the best decisions as to product profitability long and short term for the division are likely to also be best for the company. On the other hand, the management and allocation of assets, distribution of the R&D effort, and many management issues relating to marketing require surveillance on the company-wide basis.

From a division standpoint, productivity is improved when all the materials are in inventory or on order with delivery schedules to assure there will be no production stoppages because of material shortages.

If the company had unlimited resources, inventories would be kept at a level so that the production losses due to shortages would be balanced in an optimum way against the cost of carrying the inventory.

While it is not always possible to balance this equation with great precision, this is what the manufacturing manager tries to do. He can bend the balance in either direction. If he gets pressure from above, which he usually does, to improving his shipments, he will be naturally inclined to lean toward larger inventories, double ordering and other devices to assure that no shortages will prevent him from getting his quota out the door by the end of the month.

But resources are limited and beyond the cost effectiveness of larger inventories is the overall corporate question of available capital and the application of available capital to inventory requirements and other corporate needs, physical plant expansion, R&D expenditures and marketing expenditures as balanced against production expenditures.

While guidelines on inventory levels can be established by corporate management, and management incentives can be worked out, I believe each manufacturing manager can do a better job if he understands the problem on the other functional areas of the company, as well as his own.

The management of accounts receivable is in many ways a similar problem. The salesman can, no doubt, often get the business easier if he can give generous payment terms to his customer. Most people are more inclined to buy something if they can pay for it sometime in the future. Here again, the cost of carrying the financing for extended payment time can to some degree be balanced against the value of the increased business, which will result from the more favorable terms. We do have arrangements to provide financing of customer payments in situations where it is justified.

Here again, what we can afford to do as a company is limited by the total resources we have available, and an understanding of the overall corporate situation should help managers in marketing make better decisions in their area of responsibility.

These are two areas, inventory management and accounts receivable management, where our people involved in management at all levels will do a better job if they understand better the overall company problem in addition to the problem in their own area of responsibility.

Our company has grown over the years under a rather specific and carefully defined management philosophy. We have tried to benefit from the experience of others but at the same time we do not always agree with the management philosophy of other companies, or with that of all scholars of management. The latter would be in fact impossible, for all scholars of management are not in agreement on all aspects of management, by any means.

We want all of our people who are moving ahead on the management ladder in HP to be exposed to what people in other companies are doing and to the best academic thinking on management. We do not believe the thinking of others should be accepted without the most careful consideration and without an actual testing in practice in our own company.

I say this for one very important reason. The way this company has been managed in the past has been reasonably successful. For this reason we must be absolutely sure before we go off in some other direction that it will, in fact, result in improved performance.

Perhaps the most important reason for this program is to encourage a better understanding of the traditional HP management philosophy. I do not propose the policies we have followed for over three decades should be continued forever without change, but I do hope we will be very careful when we do make a change, to be sure it will be for the better.

There is another very important reason for this program. It is to encourage all of our management people to be more aware of what is going on in the outside world.

When Bill and I started the company back in 1939, there were very few restrictions on business and industry imposed by the outside world. We spent the first six months or so doing business in a residential area of Palo Alto. The government forms and reports could all be handled by my wife, working in her spare time. That would not be possible today.

Today there is hardly any action that can be taken by a manager, which is not prescribed in some way by governmental regulations. It is essential for every manager to understand these restrictions on what can be done. Some are not well defined and some can involve personal liability of serious consequence. There will be discussion of some of these matters during this week, but continuous study and awareness is essential to avoid problems, which could become serious, both for the company and for the individual managers.

At the same time, regulations by various governmental agencies are in a continual state of flux. New laws are being passed and old ones are modified by decision of the courts. There is, therefore, an ongoing opportunity for people at the management level in business and industry to have some influence on how these regulatory matters may develop in the future.

I hope there will be some discussion of this issue during the week. What can we do to influence in a constructive way new legislation that has an impact on business and industry?

I would now like to outline some of the specific management policies and philosophies, which have been in some degree responsible for our success in the past, and which I believe will serve us well in the future.

Our basic statement of corporate objectives provides the foundation for our management policies and philosophy. I believe these objectives have served their purpose well in the past and will continue to do so in the future. They have been changed very little over the years – some changes in wording and in emphasis, but no basic change in substance.

I think it is fortunate that we have had a rather constant set of rules for our management people. But these corporate objectives cover a wide range of management activities and they are certainly not perceived to mean the same thing to all people. That is why they must be continuously discussed and interpreted in relation to specific management actions. I want to discuss these objectives and make some specific points today, which I hope, will encourage discussion during the week. What is important is not how Bill and I see these objectives, but how you see them and whether you and all other management people in the company see them in essentially the same way.

Profit

In our latest statement of corporate objectives the first is Profit. I have alluded to some management areas affecting profit, which need attention.

Profits can be used in two different ways to finance growth. The first is on a pay as you go basis – resources to build the company from a direct reinvestment of profits. The second way is to use profits to attract investment, either through equity investment or debt, which must be financed with future profits.

In some industries, those which require very large capital investments, the pay as you go approach is not possible. There is also a school of thought that the capital needs should be obtained by leveraging profits and equity financing with large amounts of debt financing.

Whatever the arguments, it is not HP policy to leverage our profits with long term debt and we want every manager at every level to know this and to act accordingly. This basic and sound approach we have used for the past thirty-five years will continue to work just as well in the future as it has in the past and I can see no possible circumstance that would justify a change.

There is a very important reason why profit was placed first on the list of our corporate objectives. To maintain a pay as you go financial policy, profit on a current basis is the most critical element. It has to come ahead of everything else.

Even though profit must come ahead of everything else, it under no circumstance can be in place of our other objectives as a company, nor our other responsibilities as managers. The achievement of all of our other objectives is dependent on meeting our profit objective. At the same time, management attention given to our other objectives will help us meet our profit objective.

Profit is not very well understood by many people, I am sure including some of our employees. It is important for each of you in dealing with our people and with the public to make the point that profit is the seed corn that keeps the economy going.

Here at HP, profit is less than 10 cents of every sales dollar and that is all we need to keep our company strong and our jobs secure. For all the industry, profit is less than 10 cents in every dollar to be sound and successful. Most people believe profits are much higher and we need to do everything we can to dispel that belief.

Pay as you go financing requires not only a reasonable level of profit, but also good management of assets, inventories, accounts receivable and capital assets, buildings and equipment. We worked on these areas very diligently last year and did a good job. I hope you will discuss these matters during the week and refresh yourselves on the management actions that are needed to keep Hewlett-Packard on a pay as you go policy.

Customers

Organization and motivation are two important management activities that apply to every area of management. When the quality of a product and its value to the customer are to be given special emphasis, it is important to have the right organization structure to do the job. Some arrangement has to be provided to make sure the features the customer will want are included in every new design. Someone must be responsible to make sure reliability and low production cost are built into the design. Someone has to be responsible to make sure plans are made and implemented for good service for the customer who buys the product. If the organization is not put together with responsibility assigned to plan ahead and to follow up to see that the various tasks get done, we will not be able to meet our objective as to customers the way we want this objective to be achieved.

It is also important to foster the right employee attitude. Every employee must realize that if the customer is not satisfied with our products there will be no job. In other words, it is the responsibility of every manager to keep all of the people in his organization properly motivated to do the best possible job for our customers.

Organization and motivation are essential ingredients in every phase of management activity, but they become increasingly important in middle and higher level management positions. I hope you will include some discussion of these matters during the week.

Personnel Affairs

Management is getting things done through people as Larry Appley has put it. This means that dealing with personnel problems is the prime responsibility of every manager at every level. When the company was much smaller we did not have a personnel department because I wanted to make sure every manager in the company dealt with his own personnel problems. I thought, and still do, that taking care of his or her people was the most important part of every management job.

We have a strong personnel department today. It has several important responsibilities. One is to make sure the best personnel policies and practices are maintained in every part of the company. Another is to provide and administer a number of services for managers at all levels. In no case is the personnel department expected to handle the manager's personnel problems – he or she must accept and handle the personnel responsibility to be a good manager.

We have some very specific objectives in relation to our employees, as I am sure you all know. This is an area where we can learn from others, including scholars on management, but we must insist that everyone at every level of management know and understand and believe in and practice the HP way of working with people who work for our company.

I believe we have done a fairly good job in maintaining our company philosophy in respect to our employees. Even so, Bill and I receive a few complaints about some of our managers' actions in relation to our people that indicate a lack of understanding about what we expect. I hope you will include some discussion this week on how a manager should work with his or her people. This is such an important aspect of management that it almost transcends everything else. It is the key to productivity, to leadership and to the continuing progress and success of our company.

Dealing with the Public

One of our corporate objectives is to manage our affairs so that we are good corporate citizens in the communities where we operate. Division managers, where an HP division is large in relation to the size of the community, have the greatest responsibility in this area of management activity. Our people have done well in recognizing and accepting this responsibility, but they have often been thrown into a situation and left to sink or swim. Because we have a number of managers who have done well in this important area we should be able to use this experience to help prepare people before they are given an assignment where dealing with the public suddenly becomes a new facet of their job. I would encourage the establishment of a course to cover this subject. It should be given by HP managers who have been through the mill, and I am sure it will be helpful to those who may be asked to assume higher levels of management responsibility in the future.

Business and industry do not have a good reputation with the general public today. A decade ago a majority of the people in this country believed that American business and industry were good. They understood that we had the best products, the best jobs, that people in the United States have the highest standard of living because of the effective working of our free enterprise economy in which the privately owned and operated company like HP is the characteristic and essential element. Today much less than a majority of the people in America believe this to be true. It is this public attitude which has brought about many new laws and governmental regulations which affect the management actions of our company today.

These laws and regulations have made the job of every manager more complex and more difficult than it was two or three decades ago. This situation will probably become worse in the future, given the punitive attitude toward business and industry in the ranks of government from the local to the federal level. I will make some suggestions about what I believe we can do to help a little later.

The first requirement this situation places on every manager at every level is that he or she must know what the law requires and strive as hard as possible to avoid any illegal act. Failure to know the law is never a defense in court and it can never be an excuse for any HP manager. We plan a series of courses on business law to make sure everyone in a management assignment knows his legal responsibilities and we will expect every manager in the company to complete this education covering legal responsibilities of management as a condition of advancement.

This increased attention to the legal constraints on management is important not only for the company, but it is also important for the individual manager, for there can be civil and indeed criminal penalties for the individual as well as for the company.

We expect our management standards at HP to be well above the minimum standards established by law. I am sure you who are here today all know this, but a few problems have shown up in the past year or two which indicate the need to reinforce the understanding of this all-important matter at all levels of management throughout the company.

It is in fact those few cases where a company official is found guilty of violating the law that contribute to the bad image of business and industry in the eyes of the public. Many times a company official has committed an illegal act without knowing it was illegal. This is unfortunate for the individual but it emphasized the need for every manager to know and keep abreast of the law.

There are a number of things we can do better to help with the public image of business. The first is to make sure the public image of our own company is as good as we can possibly make it and that we do a more effective job in telling our story.

I do not propose that we undertake any new program of corporate advertising to tell the world how good we are. I do not think that would do much good anyway. I believe it will be more effective to tell our story in a personal way whenever we can through speeches to local groups, articles about what we are doing that we are proud about. I would encourage you to discuss this subject among yourselves this week. This is an area where we have maintained a low profile in the past, but I believe it is time we did a bit more.

We have already begun to take a more active part in trying to get our story over to the Congress in a more effective way. Jack Beckett has the responsibility to manage this area, which is rather new for our company. I will be speaking to a delegation of Western Congressmen at lunch in Washington tomorrow. We may not have time this week to discuss this question further of how we can develop a better understanding of our company and its role in the free enterprise system in the Congress. If not, we will certainly want to include this subject in our future management development programs and courses.

In Conclusion

I have covered some of the subjects, which I hope will be discussed during the course this week. There may be some other areas, which you think are important and should be included in the future. The objective of this program is to improve the quality of management at HP for the future. This can only be done by the education and self-improvement of you people who are taking this course this week and by everyone else in a management responsibility here at HP.

Finally, while management skill is essential to handle important areas of responsibility in the company, it is also important that every manager have a good grasp on the substance of what he is responsible to manage. Every manager must "know the territory" as the salesman says. No manager in my view can do a god job at the divisional level if he does not know all about his products, all about his customers, all about his competitors. I do not agree with those who say a good manager can manage anything. I believe, especially in a field of high technology such as ours, every manager must really know the business he is managing – management skills is not enough – every manager, if he is any good, must also "know his territory".

I hope to meet with you for a discussion the last day of the program next week. I will be particularly interested in hearing your assessment of this week's course and having your recommendations on how we can make the program better for the future.

Chapter 7

A Management Code of Ethics

"….Today's business manager must add to this heritage, not merely use it. He can best do this by first realizing that profit is not the proper end and aim of management, but only that which makes all of the proper ends and aims possible." [13]

Dave Packard

---

[13] "A Management Code of Ethics," by Dave Packard, 1/24/58. (Courtesy of Agilent Technologies Inc. Archives)

A Management Code of Ethics [14]

by
Dave Packard
(Written January 24, 1958)

The strength of the American economy system – in fact the eventual defeat of Communism – very probably will be determined by the solidarity and effectiveness of this country's business and industrial community.

We need to remind ourselves of this from time to time because of the obvious importance of successfully meeting the responsibility.

For many years the broader social responsibilities of business and industry went either unnoticed or unheeded. Not until World War II was there any noticeable effort by business and industrial leaders to accept their rightful role in local, national and foreign affairs – outside of normal business activity. During the first 40 or 50 years of this century the great majority of managers had one over-riding objective in the conduct of their businesses. That objective was to make a profit.

There is nothing wrong with profits. In fact, everything is wrong without them. But too many managers for too long seemed unmindful of the vast influence they wielded. These

---

[14] "A Management Code of Ethics," by Dave Packard, 1/24/58. (Courtesy of Agilent Technologies Inc. Archives)

men were what Herbert Hoover called the rugged individualists. He once described them as "self-reliant, rugged, God-fearing people of indomitable courage. They were the ones who asked only for freedom of opportunity and an equal chance. They gave America a genius that distinguished our people from any other in the world."

These men shaped and guided the business and industrial force of America. They have given us a rich and valuable heritage.

Today's business manager must add to this heritage, not merely use it. He can best do this by first realizing that profit is not the proper end and aim of management, but only that which makes all of the proper ends and aims possible.

Evolution of social progress is achieved in three ways. One is a build-up of countervailing forces of power. The union movement is one example, the civil rights movement another. A second mechanism is the intervention of a super authority, such as our federal government.

The third, and most constructive mechanism is one where the people in a position to improve a social situation, do so by a process of self-enlightened action.

It appears that within the past 10 or 15 years a large section of American management has acknowledged the superiority of the latter method, has begun adjusting to the concept, and has, in some cases, made an attempt to disclose this new posture to the various publics with which it deals.

Many of these men and women are following personal convictions, or ethics, in the conduct of their firm's internal and external affairs. Sometimes these codes are informal and highly individualistic. Other times they are formal and reflect a collective performance. In either case, they are valuable and effective.

The American Management Association has long encouraged the adoption of statements of ethics, and has in fact assisted many companies develop creeds. In effect they have helped build codes of ethics out of the personal ethics of the modern manager.

A code of ethics is a code of conduct not imposed by law, not imposed by common custom, but self-imposed because you believe in it. It comes from a belief in some higher selfless spirit and is directed toward the achievement of a high objective. Individuals can and of course, do have ethics and yet it is only when a large number of individuals join under a common code that high objectives are likely to be achieved. Individual businesses have codes of ethics, many of them quite adequate, yet the fulfillment of the objectives, which they seek, will be attained only when and if the large majority of business management can join together under a common code.

The great ethic, around which Western Civilization has developed, is the Judaic-Christian Code. It comes presumably from divine authority and has the highest objective for its individual adherents… a place in heaven for eternity.

But more important, at least for our discussion today, it has a high worldly objective, the brotherhood of man. The great accomplishments of the free world comes from its broad acceptance. The theme is common for all, whether it be expressed as the "Golden Rule," the "The Commandments," the "Sermon on the Mount" or from the teaching of the Talmud. It has had a tremendous achievement in a worldly sense, that all of those things which we cherish in our Western Civilization have come from the common acceptance of this code throughout the Western world.

And let us never overlook the fact that the rapid spread of Communism comes not from the ruthless power of its dictatorship, but rather from the Communistic ethic. This also contains the two essential elements – a high selfless goal, and the common acceptance of this goal by great numbers of people. We cannot accept their ideas, and we continually refuse to believe so many people do. We assume, and naturally hope, their system will fall when their dictatorship is destroyed.

We can hope that our Strategic Air Command and our missiles will deter them from starting a war – or if one starts, will enable us to defeat them before they destroy us. We are using a tremendous portion of our productive effort to build and maintain a position of strength. Yet we fail to see that the final decision will be made in our favor only if the vast majority of their people come to accept our ethic as preferable to theirs.

We can look closer at hand at the smaller units in our society – the Rotarians, the Kiwanians, all of the service and fraternal organizations, the Boy Scouts and other youth organizations – nearly every organization in this country has grown around its own code of ethics based generally, of course, upon the Judaic-Christian Code. All are directed toward high principle, in each case having broad acceptance and without question resulting in many substantial achievements.

It seems strange indeed, then, that the great fraternity of business management as a whole has not, until just recently, developed a code of ethics of more common acceptance. It is not only strange but it is unfortunate because no other group in the country with a common interest has so much influence over so many people. Our influence cuts across party lines, its extent knows no race, color or creed. We affect, in fact control, every media of mass communication. We continue to stick to the proposition that we are in business primarily to make a profit. There are some very good reasons for this in the very nature of a corporation. As managers, we are agents of our stockholders, they invest in our businesses to make a profit. We have a responsibility to do this for them, and we can point with pride at our achievements – our record in producing goods and services that has raised the standard of living in this country to a level almost beyond belief.

There are signs that even in 1958 American business has not quite measured up in the eyes of the world. Recently a group of business managers thought it might be helpful to discuss some of the current problems of society with representatives of other professions. At one such meeting, in this case with a group of ministers, the business managers were enthusiastic in presenting their philosophy, and in describing what they were doing to improve the total society environment.

One of the ministers obviously was becoming more and more puzzled as the discussion went along, and finally the chairman asked him, "Is there something you don't understand?" The minister's reply was, "Yes, I am confused by the enthusiasm you have for business management. You seem to indicate you are interested in social welfare and in many things other than profit. I thought business management was the practice of exploiting labor simply to make a profit."

We also know from experience that people overseas like our products but question our ethics.

We in private industry have much to do to improve the image others have of us, but the image is less important than the performance.

Perhaps translation of our own personal codes of ethics into our management jobs is not enough. If we are to assume the rather awesome social responsibilities we have at home and abroad, perhaps we need to develop a clear-cut management code of ethics, which can stand on its own and be accepted on a broad basis by all business people.

There seems to be little doubt that business and industrial management must rise above the materialistic objective of producing goods and services and profits.

One of the reasons we have not done this is because we have not yet agreed upon a higher aim – the basis for any true code of ethics.

We in business management do indeed have a higher aim – the preservation of our freedom on which to base a code of ethics. You can be sure that the production of goods and services will go on in this country whether or not we have a free enterprise system.

As a suggestion, here are a few tenets that might be considered for a management code. These are not one man's ideas. They come from statements business leaders have made over the past several years.

One tenet is to manage our business enterprises first and foremost so we make a contribution to society. If we provide a service, it should be the best possible service, oriented toward the public welfare. If we make a product, it should represent the utmost in quality and value. This is, of course, precisely what the most successful businesses do.

Another tenet is to recognize the dignity and personal worth of every person we employ. In subscribing to this tenet, we must provide an opportunity for employees to share in the company's success, provide them job security based on job performance, and most importantly, recognize their need for personal satisfaction that comes from a sense of accomplishment.

This concept has achieved some acceptance. It must be emphasized that the objective of this proposed tenet is not simply to make our organizations more efficient, although this will certainly be one result. This ethic, however we choose to express it, must be based solidly on the premise that labor is not a commodity to be bought and sold in the marketplace.

The third tenet has to be with management's responsibility to society at large. Our churches and schools play a great part in the intellectual and moral training on which we rely every day and rarely give a second thought. Many of the tools and techniques we use in our day-to-day work have emanated from the efforts of our great universities in extending the frontiers of knowledge.

We have a responsibility for our private charities. Not only should we provide them money from our businesses and encourage our employees to give them support, be we should also participate actively in the establishment and achievement of their goals. Whenever possible, social welfare should be the responsibility of privately supported institutions.

The forth tenet in our code should be directed toward a better understanding of the nature of profit. Profit is the monetary measurement of our contribution to society. It is the difference between the value of the goods and services we give to society, and the value we take from it. Profit is the insurance we have that our business will continue to grow and flourish. With a good profit we can meet our obligations to our customers, to employees, and to the public at large. We can also provide our stockholders with a fair return to encourage their continued investment as well. And, most importantly, it is the wherewithal we need to assist in the furtherance of man's progress.

Last year I attended a meeting of business and industrial leaders, a good cross-section of business leadership. For two days these men discussed how they and their firms could strengthen and broaden their contribution to social progress. They discussed how they could aid education, how they could help the government --- national, state, local – do a better job. They discussed business influence in international affairs, how they could help in solving the problems of automation, and many other broad social problems, including how they could advance civil rights.

They all believe, of course, that an adequate profit is necessary for a business to grow and flourish in our free enterprise economy. But that subject was not mentioned.

Those attending the conference agreed that this is a century of science, but they indicated by their thoughts that this is also a century of social and political progress.

The contribution of the business community to this progress is gradually increasing. But the weight of our contribution will not be felt until we recognize that final and permanent change for the better in all human affairs comes not from strife between people, or groups of people attempting to force acceptance of their views; not from power imposed by a super authority; but rather from self-enlightened action of all concerned – whether they be individuals or nations. This is the challenge and the responsibility of the free society, it is the challenge and the responsibility of American business management as well.

A management code of ethics can provide direction of purpose, and significantly enough, at the same time provide an essential ingredient in the bonding and unification of the business community – a unification so necessary to the advancement of American business, the American economic and political system, and a free world.

The Russians have demonstrated they can produce products without profits and without liberty. We are on trial before the world to prove we can produce products and services for a better life, with profits and with liberty.

<u>*Chapter 8*</u>

Social Responsibilities

"...while I have pointed out that business has come a long way in developing a social conscience, let me assure you that it still has a long way to go.." [15]

Dave Packard

---

[15] "Business as a Social Institution," by Dave Packard, 5/6/66. (Courtesy of Agilent Technologies Inc. Archives)

Business as a Social Institution [16]

by

Dave Packard

America Heritage Lecture Series

University of Colorado, Boulder, Colorado

(May 6th, 1966)

We are continuing to experience the most impressive period of economic prosperity and growth in the history of America. In statistical terms, our production of goods and services, as measured by the gross national product calculation, has grown from a rate of 504 billion dollars in 1960 to an estimated 725 billion $ in 1966.

To put these figures in perspective, in a mere five years we have increased our output of goods and services by an amount nearly equal to the total goods and services available to the people in France and Germany combined. In terms of the total goods and services available in America, this is an increase of over 40%. If we make adjustments for population growth, which has been substantial, and inflation, which is less significant, the average American has 17% more of the material things in life than he had five years ago.

The future looks equally bright. Although there is increasing concern about the specter of inflation, the economy remains

---

[16] "Business as a Social Institution," by Dave Packard, 5/6/66. (Courtesy of Agilent Technologies Inc. Archives)

very strong, and is likely to continue to grow at a rapid rate over the foreseeable future. One might conclude from these circumstances that the millennium is here – that our society has every reason to be both proud and content about its progress, and with its accomplishments. Yet, with this widespread and growing affluence there is a strong current of restlessness, a growing concern among the American people about our society. It is a concern among groups of people who feel they have not received their fair share of the increasing prosperity. But, it is also the concern of people who believe that a society should provide more than material benefits to its people. It is expressed by students who, in the long history of our country, have never had a greater opportunity to acquire a good education. It is expressed by men and women in government, in professional life, in the arts, in business and industry. It is a basic questioning of our goals and values – and it is expressed by many thinking Americans.

It is true that a great deal of this evident social unrest is expressed by minority groups of various kinds. Recent studies of the student demonstrations in our universities indicate that only a small minority of the total student body takes an active role in the demonstrations and a few more go along just for the "kicks." But the great majority of students are just as serious and well behaved and conventional as their parents had been in school – perhaps even more so.

Even on such a major issues as civil rights, only a small, although vocal, minority is concerned enough to take an active part. But the fact that only a minority participates by no means diminishes the fact that there is increasing concern among our people about their society. New ideas are generated by individuals, not crowds, and new trends are always led by minority groups.

It is not easy to keep things in the proper perspective, especially when they are going on all around us. For this reason it is difficult to keep the current upsurge of social unrest in perspective. The age-old American Dream of social equality, and a good life for every American, has generated a turmoil, which has been recorded, in varying degrees of intensity, in every period of our history. If the turmoil seems greater today it may be because communication between people is more efficient than ever before, with radio, television, easy and rapid travel across the country, in addition to the written word in newspapers, periodicals and books.

Even though the present social unrest is expressed in the main by minorities, and its manifestations are magnified by our vast and efficient communication facilities, it seems nevertheless a very real and genuine phenomenon. Behind it lays the immensely important fact that the great economic progress of the Western World has brought legitimate social goals with reach of all. Under these circumstances it seems to me that impatience with progress – or rather, the lack of progress – is bound to increase.

Social equalities were, after all, one of the founding concepts of America. It represented the opportunity to improve one's position, to provide a better life for one's children. This concept was interpreted largely in economic terms during the early years of our history. The American Dream was developed in an environment, which rewarded hard work and ability, rather than social background. The proper rewards were a better job, a better home, a better economic position, when the majority were living at the edge of poverty. But it is taking a shortsighted view of human nature, indeed, to assume that aspirations are, or should be, limited to the benefits of affluence. An improved economic status is a reasonable first objective in human progress, but it should by no means be considered the only, or the final, objective.

It seems to me, then, quite reasonable to assume that as satisfactory levels of material well-being are achieved, other goals and aspirations of people will become more important. Were it otherwise, a society would pursue a certain course from poverty to affluence to decadence. Furthermore, as a large majority of our people achieve a satisfactory economic position, those who fail to do so are properly more concerned as to why they are left behind.

Thus, while I do not always agree with the methods which have developed in some areas of our current social unrest, while I am concerned by some of the disruptive forces behind them, I must conclude that the developments are logical and healthy for the future of America.

This concern about America and its future is apparent in every facet of our society. It is being expressed in the government by a myriad of new laws and administrative action directed toward social welfare. It is being expressed by the churches, no longer content with the role of leading the way to a better life in the hereafter. They are increasingly becoming involved in trying to make a better life here, now. New organizations to attack social problems are springing up on every side. The institution of business is not exempt from these influences – in fact, the business community is very much at the forefront of the modern social revolution. Today I want to explore with you some of the developments which have been changing the business enterprise from a strictly economic activity to an activity which has a strong social basis, and one which is having, and will continue to have, profound effect on the progress of our society in other than material ways.

The business community has, almost throughout history, been accused of crass, materialistic, selfish motives. In the words of Dr. Samuel Johnson, 200 years ago – "A merchant's desire is not of glory but of gain, not of public wealth but of private involvement: he is rarely to be consulted on questions of war or peace, or any designs of wide extent and distant consequence." And long before that, the moneychangers were driven from the temple.

In more modern times it has been widely accepted that the business of business is business – and nothing else. The capitalistic, free enterprise, business community of America has traditionally defended itself in this position – by claiming, and with ample justification, that its methods have produced for the American Society the highest standard of living the world has ever known.

Before the turn of the century the profit motive and free enterprise were sometimes defended on the theory of selective and self-improving evolution – the survival of the fittest. After all, this is a fundamental law of nature. As John D. said in defending the Standard Oil monopoly:

"The growth of a large business is merely a survival of the fittest. The American Beauty Rose can be produced in the splendor and fragrance, which brings cheer to its beholder, only by sacrificing the early buds, which grow up around it. This is not an evil tendency in business, it is merely the working out of a law of nature and of God."

Throughout the early decades of the twentieth century, the profit motive and a laissez faire economic environment were the ingredients, which continued to build strength into the American economy, and an improved standard of living for its people. Business leaders could point with justifiable pride to their accomplishments. The average standard of living in America advanced at an impressive rate. The door was always open for a person with ambition, ability, and a little luck, to move up the ladder – often two rungs at a time. The Horatio Alger story was repeated frequently enough to make it a credible goal for any young man or young woman. And it remains so today.

But with all of this impressive economic progress, and with the great opportunity for upward economic and social mobility, which the American free enterprise business system provided, there has been a growing, disquieting concern that this was not enough. Even before the turn of the century it was clear that the American society expected a broader responsibility from its business community. The government expressed its expectations with laws to control trusts, to protect consumers and employees. Labor unions expanded, often led by men who felt they had been denied opportunities in industry. In time they became a formidable counter-force to the power of business.

The concern of the public about business practice, as expressed through its government, unions, and consumer groups, was intensified by every depression, and the great depression of the 1930's was no exception. When the economy was strong, it seemed reasonable to argue that the harsh practices, which resulted from uncontrolled free enterprise and the profit motive, were a small price to pay for the great economic progress produced. When the economy collapsed, the argument collapsed, and the critical attention of public opinion came to action. Thus the New Deal added new constraints to business, and the power of labor expanded throughout the thirties.

The growth of business regulation by law, and the growth of union power, were not without their effect on the attitude of business leaders. Throughout the first part of the century there was a growing awareness that business managers did, in fact, have a responsibility beyond making a profit for their investors. They became more aware that their responsibility to their customers was not limited to the doctrine of caveat emptor. They began to realize that labor was not a commodity to be bought and sold on the open market, but was composed of men and women with human aspirations, and should be treated accordingly.

This trend toward a greater social awareness on the part of business was encouraged by the development of Scientific Management. The roots of Scientific Management go deep in American history. The American system of manufacture began to evolve in the early 19th century. Interchangeable parts, the beginning of mass production, was introduced by Eli Whitney in 1800. Special apparatus adapted to a single operation, attention to plant layout and material handling, were used in early manufacturing industries. F. W. Taylor's techniques, which began with time and motion studies, were directed at improving production efficiency, and provided the basis for a management profession. This new profession was limited to specialists in its early years. Out of this beginning has grown a group of people well trained in the expertise of management, who have largely replaced the entrepreneur as the business leader.

Taylor predicted this development in 1911 when he wrote: "In the past the prevailing idea has been well expressed in the saying that 'Captains of Industry are born, not made. In the future it will be appreciated that our leaders must be trained right, as well as born right.'"

An interesting study of Elton Moyo, of Harvard, brought into focus the "human relations" in management. In a famous experiment at the Western Electric Company, he found that people responded to an improved environment with improved productivity. More important, his experiment seemed to demonstrate that people performed better if someone is simply interested in their welfare. This was a revolutionary idea in the 1920's, but we see it work every day in our factories through out the country in 1966.

Market research brought the needs and desires of the customer into focus. The case of the Model T Ford clearly demonstrated that the business manager who thought he alone should decide what the customer should have would be left behind. This lesson did not go by unheeded by business leaders. Despite all the talk about "hidden persuaders" the customer today is a very sophisticated person. No business can survive for long unless it serves its customers well.

And throughout the past few decades business people have taken an increasing interest in the community around them. This was first expressed by the private philanthropy of men who had achieved wealth through their business careers. They built libraries and schools, and contributed in other ways to the public benefit. Then business organizations began to provide support for the social and cultural activities in the communities where they were located. This trend was greatly accelerated by the New Jersey court decision in A. P. Smith Mfg. Vs. Barlow case in 1953, which established that it was a proper function for a corporation to contribute to the support of education and other social endeavors. In recent years business support of America's schools, colleges and universities has grown at a rapid rate, reaching a level of some $300,000,000 in 1965. Most private universities depend on such support as a major factor in sustaining their current academic programs. In addition, they enjoy the use of thousands of classrooms, laboratories and libraries, which have been provided by the business community of America. Many of the young men and women in school today are supported by scholarships and fellowships provided by American business. Sometimes this has been done by business people to attract bright young people to their organizations. More recently it has been done because business leaders have felt a responsibility on a broad base to the welfare of society.

The attitude of business leadership has come a long way since that day, eighty-some years ago, when William Henry Vanderbilt told a couple of Chicago reporters, "The public be damned!"

It didn't matter that Vanderbilt later denied it, or insisted that he'd been quoted out of context. It was not Vanderbilt per se who put "the public be damned" into the record books – public opinion did. Because, as far as that same public was concerned, his words defined the attitude prevailing among the business leaders of the 1880's.

Were Vanderbilt around today he would discover, perhaps to his dismay, that business has become an important social institution.

Perhaps it is more accurate to say it has become a constructive social institution. Ever since the evolution of the industrial economy, business has had an important influence, in one way or another, on the personal lives of many people.

The jobs, which are provided by the business community, supply the sole source of income for a majority of all families. One might conclude, if this income is adequate for a reasonable standard of living, the responsibility of business is satisfied. This, however, overlooks the fact that most people spend a large portion of their waking hours at their job. For this reason it has always seemed to me that the working environment, the satisfaction – the enjoyment, if you will – a person received from the work he does, is important. And I think most business managers, the people who determine such things, have come to agree.

I am always impressed as I travel around the country and visit new industrial plants, new industrial parks, and see the extent to which these have been made more attractive. The progress is most impressive when I recall the dirty, unattractive industrial sections I used to ride through on the train going into Chicago twenty years ago.

When one sees the inside of these new, modern factories, the comparison with factories built a few decades ago is even more impressive. In our company we have gone to great lengths to make our plants as attractive as possible for our people, with good lighting, attractive colors, air conditioning, and recreation areas for us in the noon hour. On more than one occasion an employee has said to me, "I look forward to coming to work every day." I am sure this experience is not unique in our company.

But it is not just the physical environment, which makes a job something more than a way to earn a wage. It is also the attitude and relationship among people in the plant. The tough, hard-boiled foreman is a thing of the past. Supervisors are trained in human relations, and many other things are done to treat employees as people, rather than as numbers on a time clock. There are company activities; clubs of numerous kinds for employees, and in every sense a job has become a part of a person's social life, as well as his economic life. I am convinced the trends toward this end will expand.

They will expand partly because they are good business. People do a better job when they are treated as human beings. These trends will expand also because business people, business managers, are becoming more sensitive to their social responsibilities.

There are many other manifestations of this growing social conscience in the business community. Some are seen in the inner workings of the enterprise, others in relations with the outside world.

There has been a great deal more attention to the customer, in quality of product and service, in recent years. This may not be as evident because neither product nor service are ever perfect, and people are quick to point out the deficiencies and failures. The drug industry seems to be a favorite whipping boy, but if you want to be objective about it, read the ads for some of the patent remedies, which were offered to the public at the beginning of the century. Look up some of the formulae, which were used then. No present day drug company would think of offering the public such concoctions – the Food and Drug Administration notwithstanding.

I do not propose to say that the business community has developed a social conscience toward the customer without some prodding by government regulations, and without the discipline of a free market. Without a doubt, the free market has been the strongest factor in encouraging a sense of business responsibility to the customers. In any case, if one thinks the customer can be protected by the government alone, I suggest he pay a short visit to Russia, where the government has been in complete control of the production of consumer products. There the public could hardly fare worse in getting what it wants and needs, either in quantity or quality.

It is in its relationship with the public-at-large that the development of a social conscience in business is most clearly seen. In this area things are happening which do not have a clearly definable business purpose. In some instances they seem even adverse in some degree to the short-term interest of the business enterprise.

Twice during the past two years the President has called on the business community to undertake voluntary action to help solve a problem of national interest. In one case he asked business to limit expenditures and investments overseas to help the country's balance of payment problem. The problem was caused primarily by government foreign aid and defense expenditures, which generated an outflow of dollars. Increasing overseas travel by the American public was also a contributing factor. The problem could have been solved by restrictions in these areas alone. The business community was already generating a substantial favorable balance of trade and dollar inflow. On request of the President, the business community undertook voluntarily to increase its favorable balance, even though this meant the loss of profits, some short-term and some long-term. This was clearly an action based largely on social responsibility, rather than business responsibility.

Just a few week ago the President asked again for the business community to take voluntary action to help stem the threat of inflation which has been developing in our economy over the past few months. A hardheaded business response to the

President would have been, "Your inflationary fiscal and political policies are generating this threat. Modify them and you can solve the problem."

A clear sense of social responsibility prevailed among the business community, however, and voluntary action has been undertaken, again at the expense of legitimate business plans and programs.

One of the most difficult problems is that of Civil Rights. There are action groups, which make the headlines. There has been considerable legislation. Behind this is a great deal of constructive effort by the business community. We are working hard to make available more jobs for minority groups. Many of the people in the minority groups have inadequate education and training for the jobs, which are available. To help in this matter most business organizations have expanded their company training programs to help people improve their abilities and to move ahead. Great emphasis is being placed on the job of improving attitudes for better acceptance of these people in their jobs. These efforts are making an important contribution toward the improvement of opportunities for under-privileged minority groups. What I see going on in the business community is more impressive, and I believe producing more progress, than all of the activities, which are reported in the headlines – the governmental activities not excepted.

Another area, broader in scope, in which the business community is making a significant contribution, is that of public affairs. This covers a wide range of community, civic and political activities. Not too many years ago, most businessmen took the attitude that "politics is none of my business – nor the business of my employees."

Today, however, we find many companies who are devoting considerable time, money and effort to encouraging their employees to take more active, personal interest in political and other civic affairs. These people are urged to participate in community activities, to contribute their services and financial support to the party of their choice, to inform themselves on issues and candidates, and, of course, to vote. This increased activity is based on the premise that the American system cannot prevail unless competent men and women lend their interest and talents to the process of self-government. Business is no longer content to "let George do it"; it has come to the realization that politics is not the politicians' business – it is everybody's business.

Week in and week out I see business people concerned with other national problems. I see them providing advice and counsel to various governmental agencies, serving on committees, doing a number of public-spirited jobs – often at a sacrifice of time and energy which could be well spent in managing their own enterprises.

Now, while I have pointed out that business has come a long way in developing a social conscience, let me assure you that it still has a long way to go. There are still within our ranks practitioners of chicanery, double-talk, fact-dodging, half-truths. There are those who are so enamored with short-term profits that they overlook the importance of building long-term strength and vitality into their organizations.

And even among those who have shown a flicker of public spirit, of responsible citizenship, there are still some who are unwilling to tackle the really big problems of the day – civil rights, mass transportation, water pollution, poverty, urban renewal. These are problems that cannot be solved by any single group of our society, but by the cooperative effort of many dedicated groups.

As an example of an area where much remains to be done, let's look at education. I mentioned that business support of education now amounts to nearly $1,000,000 per day. This is an enormous outlay, and one of which the business community is justifiably proud. But simply turning over a check to his favorite school or college does not end the businessman's responsibility to education. He needs to find out how the money is spent, how our schools and colleges can do a better job of developing America's most important resource – our many millions of younger people.

We spend a great deal of time talking about how our colleges and universities can improve their curricula. And the business community expends considerable effort in checking grade-point averages and enticing the brightest young men and women into their organizations.

But what of the fifty percent of our younger people who will never get to college?   These people, many of whom are employable and certainly trainable, are in many cases being shunted off into the wings.   As Peter Drucker, the noted business writer and lecturer, has pointed out, there is a real danger that our country will be divided by the "paper curtain" of the college diploma.   This is a political and social danger – and I think an economic danger.   It certainly is, or should be, the concern of every business leader to create opportunities for the non-college graduate and to see that he is not considered an object of charity.   It also should be a concern of businessmen to work with educators at all levels of our school system – from the first grade on up – to see that we are getting the most for our educational dollar.

Without belaboring the point, let me just say that we have a long way to go in education.   And education is only one thread in the fabric of American life, one of many problems to which the business community must apply itself if we are to build a more meaningful, constructive society.

It has been pointed out that the business leader, in attempting to improve the quality of our society, is sometimes confronted with conflicting pressures.   On one hand is the responsibility to his stockholders and employees to optimize profits.   On the other hand, his efforts to upgrade the social environment may, in fact, penalize profits.

Actually, in my judgment there is little conflict between a corporation's social responsibility and its economic responsibility to its stockholders. And what little conflict exists is focused on the short-term, rather than the longer, broader gauged view of return-on-investment.

While stockholders expect the corporation to earn a profit today, they also expect it to create and enhance an environment in which it can continue to earn a profit tomorrow. George Champion, chairman of the Chase Manhattan Bank, summed up this concept rather well when he recently stated:

'Business must learn to look upon its social responsibilities as something inseparable from its economic function. Since private enterprise has an important bearing upon the lives, aspirations and future well-being of the people, it has a corresponding obligation to contribute to the solution of their economic and social problems. If it fails to do so, it leaves a void that will quickly be filled by others – usually by government."

In the course of these remarks I have emphasized that business has come a long way from the laissez faire, profit-motivated attitude which prevailed at the turn of the century. But I don't wish to imply that freedom of business decision and profit making are no longer important. These, in fact, remain the mainspring of our entire economic system. The myriad of decisions necessary for a vigorous, growing economy cannot be effectively made from a central authority. Rather they must be formulated with the business community itself, operating in the framework of a free and competitive market.

It is my firm conviction that this same freedom of decision by business management is a powerful force in over-coming the great social problems confronting America. Legislation can provide a guide to social betterment, and action groups may add to the incentive, but the real progress comes from the day-to-day decisions of those people directly involved. To a very large extent these are the thousands of business leaders throughout the country.

But social progress is impossible without economic progress; therefore social progress will be made only if we continue to have a healthy, growing economy. In our free enterprise system, economic health and vitality are, in the final analysis, determined and measured by profit. Today we consider profit not just as a return on the investment made in a business, but as the best single measure of the contribution a business makes to the society in which it exists. And the profit a business makes is, in final analysis, the sole source of its strength to grow, to provide more and better jobs, to do its share in helping to create a better life for its employees, for its customers, and for the public-at-large, as well as for those people who invest and risk their money in the business.

The preservations of free enterprise is by far the most important pillar of the Great Society which we all hope to attain as we move on into the future.

Business Management and Social Responsibilities [17]

by

Dave Packard

Children's Home Society of California

(May 17th, 1965)

I am pleased to have the privilege of being with you this evening. It is a special pleasure to be able to join you in honoring my good friend, Dr. Edward Liston, as your new state chairman.

I am also glad to have this opportunity to congratulate you, as members of the Children's Home Society of California, for the long and valuable contribution you have made to the welfare of the California community. In establishing an all-time high of 1,273 children placed in permanent adoption homes last year, you have given ample evidence of the important leadership which private charitable organizations contribute to the social welfare of America.

The good work you are doing is made possible, in large measure, by the volunteer work each of you has contributed. If it were possible to assess the value of the talent, the time, and the devoted interest, which is involved in a private charitable institution such as yours, I am sure it would far exceed the value

---

[17] "Business Management and Social Responsibilities," by Dave Packard, 5/17/65. (Courtesy of Agilent Technologies Inc. Archives)

of the monetary contributions you receive from your benefactors.

Private endeavors for the benefit of society have a long and honorable tradition in the history of the Western world. Our earliest, and some of our most distinguished, educational institutions began from – and still depend on – private initiative.

Many other important institutions devoted to the well being of people were founded, as was yours, because an individual was concerned about the welfare of his fellow citizens.

In many cases, segments of the responsibility for social welfare have been taken over by government bodies. We see this on the national, state, and local levels. There has evolved over the years in the United States, a unique blending of private and government efforts.

Much of the involvement of the government has come about as a result of the magnitude of the job to be accomplished. Education, for example, is an area so comprehensive and complex that it is hard to imagine the system minus the governmental role.

And yet, we find private schools and universities still holding positions of great importance. They have a unique position of leadership because they can concentrate on quality – they have the freedom and flexibility to nurture innovation – they can institute special programs, devote individual attention to outstanding students, and often develop areas of excellence which are difficult – or impossible – for public supported institutions to match.

This is not to say that public schools are without accomplishment. They are doing a good job, too. Having been closely involved with the field of education over the past number of years, I am convinced that our pluralistic approach has given us educational opportunities for our young people far superior to those found anywhere else in the world.

There are many other important, and special, areas of our society where government agencies look to private organizations for leadership and standards of excellence. This is certainly true in the case of your society, as we see examples of public agencies striving to meet your achievements in finding good homes for the unfortunate youngsters who are born without that privilege.

But unfortunately, during the past few years we have seen a growing number of critics of private endeavor. We have been bombarded with books such as "The Hidden Persuaders," "The Organization Man," "The Status Seekers," and "Life in the Crystal Palace," just to name a few. These books, and others, are focusing their attention on the business community – but the private charitable organization is under attack as well.

To give a recent example, in his 1964 annual report of the Carnegie Corporation, John Garner outlines very well the nature of some of these current threats to private charity. The attack, as he points out, is aimed at the tax deductibility of charitable contributions, and at the very existence of charitable foundations – on which much of our private social benefits depend.

The argument goes that because tax money actually belongs to the government, when an individual receives a tax deduction for his gift, he is in fact giving away the government's money not his own. Those presenting this argument include the Socialists who believe everything can be done better by the government.

Essentially, the same arguments are used against private foundations. They insist that the wealth an individual is able to accumulate in his lifetime should not be used for purposes he selects, such as the establishment of a charitable foundation. This money, too, they say, belongs to the government.

The critics of foundations have received some support for their arguments by the fact that some trust administrations have been abused. But, the fact remains that the institutions of private charity and private enterprise are under unnecessary attack, and vigilance is required to do that.

However, it is not necessary to use common <u>dangers</u> to support the proposition that private charity has much in common with the private business community. There are enough common <u>goals</u> and ideals to do that.

John Garner used the words "private initiative for the common good" to define the private charity, and I believe that it is as good a definition as I have ever heard to also define the motives and aspirations of the modern business manager.

I emphasize the word <u>modern</u> because this would not have been an accurate description of management motivation in general before the first half of the 20th century. In the last few decades there has been a great change in the business management profession.

I can clearly recall my own experiences 15 or 20 years ago discussing management problems with business people, when the prevailing view was that the primary objective of the management function was to make a profit. Employee relations were directed toward maintaining production and profit, without regard for the social consequences. The concept that labor was a commodity to be bought and sold on the open market prevailed. Involvement in community or pubic affairs was measured in terms of the specific benefits it would buy. "Caveat emptor" still persisted in dealing with customers.

In the years preceding World War II, some progress had been made in the development of social responsibility in business management, but the concept of "what's good for business is good for the country" still prevailed to a large degree. There were, during these years, business managers who felt differently about their responsibilities. They had recognized, and honored, the view that every employee is a human being – that he has his aspirations, his home, and his family – and that in making his contribution to his job he deserved consideration beyond the mechanical payment of an hourly or daily wage. Had more managers realized this sooner, there would have been little need for the unions to take up the battle on behalf of the workers of that day.

Some managers were also beginning to recognize that they had a broader responsibility to the communities in which their business were established than could be defined on a "quid pro quo" basis. They realized that their enterprises were an integral part of the society at large and that they did in fact have a responsibility to make sure their organizations were good corporate citizens.

These same managers realized that they had a mandate to give their customers the best products, and the best services, that could be produced. They had come to the conclusion that the seller had a responsibility to make sure the buyer did not have to beware.

The exacting disciplines of competition contributed toward these ends, but it took more than competition – it required a new attitude on the part of management.

During the years since World War II, this new attitude has come to a high state of maturity. It has a strong effect on the people who make up the management profession today. It is beginning to become an accepted and expected philosophy by the general public.

The president of one of the nation's largest business organizations a few years back put it this way: "As citizens, people expect not only the kind of material performance that contributes toward a prosperous economy and the national security. They also look to a company to measure up to their ethical and social expectations, and represented by such things as its genuine interest in people and the community – its emphasis on human considerations – its really dedicated work in charity and other worthwhile causes – its obedience both in the spirit and the letter of the law – and its recognition that what other people think is important. In other words, over and above material performance, the people expect business to help achieve their personal aspirations, and the permanent aspirations that are associated with the United States of America."

The old manager didn't recognize these responsibilities. In most cases he was the owner as well as manager – he had learned his job in the school of hard knocks – he had a minimum amount of formal education – and he struggled to survive in a rough and tumble world.

These managers were the rugged individualists which Herbert Hoover described on several occasions during the months preceding his election nearly 40 years ago, as "self-reliant, rugged, God-fearing people of indomitable courage." They were the one who asked only for freedom of opportunity and an equal chance.   They gave to America a genius that distinguished our people from any other in the world."

He continued this theme in one of his books written in 1934 when he said, "While I cannot claim having introduced the term "rugged individualism", I should be proud to have invented it. It has been used by American leaders for over a half-century in eulogy of those God-fearing men and women of honesty whose stamina, and character, and fearless assertion of rights, led them to make their own way in life."

These words of Mr. Hoover's describe very eloquently the type of men and women who shaped and guided the business and industrial force of America.   They were the managers of a yesteryear.

Today's manager has this heritage, but he has become more of a professional.   The great majority of them have had the same extensive, formal educations held by lawyers, ministers, doctors, and other professional people.   In fact, some have been professors before going into industry and business.   Their attitudes toward the community at large should be no different than any other representative group of Americans.

I have had the unique opportunity during the past few years of becoming well acquainted with a large number of the top managers of American business. These men are just as aware – and just as concerned with the problems of our society at large, as any other group of Americans. The meetings they hold are not just to discuss how they can improve their profits – are not for the purpose of scheming against the government – but rather to discuss how they, as representatives of their companies, and as individuals, can help to build a better America.

They are firm believers in, and standard bearers for, the free enterprise system, of course. They know they must manage their organizations to make a profit. But – and this is the crux of the management philosophy of our age – they look on profit as a measure of the contribution their organizations are making to society, and on free enterprise as the vehicle essential for achieving the social aspirations of all of the people.

Let me quote a few words from Mr. E.J. Hamley, chairman and president of Allegheny Ludlum Steel, as just one example of modern management thinking. In a recent talk, he first cited some of the material accomplishments of the American business community. Then he went on to say:

"With all this accomplishment we would think that the responsibility of the business world, and the individual businessman might have ended at the office door. But this is not so. For, to a greater degree today than ever, business and businessmen are expected now to have a great and growing interest in general community welfare. And, happily, American business generally exhibits just such an interest in a magnificent fashion."

We have come a long way from Mr. Hoover's rugged individualist. Today's professional manager is not quite so rugged as he was a few decades ago, but fortunately he is still something of an individualist. With all of his added responsibilities, he still provides the essential motivation and drive, which makes the American economy the envy of the world.

I cannot conclude my argument that modern business managers have a genuine social responsibility without a few specific comments about the role they have played in the very important task of providing more and better goods and services for the American people – a performance that far exceeds that of any other economic system.

A few years ago, particularly during Khrushchev's happy days, we heard a great deal about the Communistic system. You will recall, he said, "We will bury you." In passing, let me remind you he was expressing the desire and intent of the Communist world – and despite what has happened since that time, this still remains the desire and intent of the Communists.

Let me tell you what has happened since 1960. In the year of 1960, our U.S. gross national product – the best measure of performance of an economy – was about 500 billion dollars. In this year of 1965, the figure will be in excess of 650 billion dollars. This is an increase of 150 billion dollars in goods and services produced by the American free enterprise system in five years.

The next largest economy in the free world today is that of West Germany, which will have a gross national product in 1965 of about 114 billion dollars. The West Germany economic system has performed the best of all of these other countries, and is the one most closely aligned with the American system, particularly with respect to the individual initiative and enthusiasm.

Even so, as you can see, we have added an amount nearly one and one-half times as large to our economy in just the past five years.

France, which under De Gaulle is acting impertinent, will have a total economy in 1965 of around 86 billion dollars. We are adding this amount to our economy every three to four years.

Great Britain has an economy only slightly larger than France. With the population about one-quarter that of the United States, they produce only about one-seventh the goods and services.

Because of the perspective it affords us, I cannot avoid the comment about the sad plight of Great Britain.

Here is a country, which once had the strongest economy in the world. Her navies ruled the seas. Her products – the epitome of quality and value – were sought throughout the world. She was the champion for the free enterprise of business.

Today, Great Britain is no longer competitive in world trade. The integrity of the pound is upheld only by the charity of her friends through the largest loans ever granted from the international monetary fund.

The spirit of her people is broken. They enjoy a wage level about a quarter of that found in America. They can't afford housing, so the government supplies it for them on a subsidized basis. They can't afford medical care, so the government provides Medicare. The whole country has forsaken free enterprise for socialism.

It is an irony of fate, I think, that the labor government – which played so large a part in sowing the seed – has now returned to reap the harvest.

There is a lesson here for us. We are being presented with the largest dose of public welfare ever received by any nation. The War on Poverty Commission has billions of dollars available to it to combat any local economic situation they can find, which might possibly improve the standard of living for a few people.

The administration seems convinced that private initiative in medical care is a failure, and that only the federal government can solve the problem.

They are convinced that education needs federal support – and if you analyze the federal education bill you will find that they intend to give this support to education in every state it is needed or not.

Under the present administration we are walking in some of the same footprints made by Great Britain. If we continue along this same path, it is bound to have the same results for us that it has had for them.

Fortunately, President Johnson still has some respect for private initiative. He has given the American free enterprise business community a good deal of support. It is the greatest show of ambivalence this country has ever seen.

I do not know whether our free enterprise economy is capable of providing the goods and services necessary for the well being of America, and at the same time supporting all the social benefits the government is proposing to distribute in the "Great Society." However, we will have a stronger and greater society if we maintain the free enterprise approach for both our desires, and his.

I firmly believe that free enterprise in social welfare is an absolute necessity to support free enterprise in business. Once social welfare becomes a government monopoly – as it is rapidly becoming – it is only a matter of time before we see it requires only another series of steps to put business under government monopoly. And then, we will be following the lead of Great Britain in moving from one of the world's greatest economies to the position of a second-rate nation. The rugged individualist will be extinct, and the responsible individual will have joined him.

But, to get back to the present economic situation, suffice it to say that in 1965 our gross national product will exceed the total of all the other countries of the free world combined.

Estimates on the economies of Russia and China are hard to come by – but I have heard reports that Russia produces something in the neighborhood of 350 billion dollars.

If we add up all the known free world economies, and the estimates for the Communist-dominated portion of the world, it is within reason to say that the United States produces some 35 to 40 percent of the world's economic strength – and all of this with some 7 percent of the world's population.

If we can preserve and strengthen our free enterprise system, there is not the slightest chance that the Communists can ever catch up with us – let alone bury us!

In light of these impressive figures, it is surprising that the image of the business manager remains so poor. At least one survey I have seen within the past few years indicated that industry generally is gaining on the government and labor in receiving a favorable vote of confidence by the public – but on the reverse side of the coin, business still holds a rather strong lead among those people who have an intense unfavorable attitude toward one of the three major categories of business, government and labor.

This same survey also showed that teen-agers tend to accept the bad stereotypes of business, and like many of their parents, see corporations as monopolistic and dangerously large. The one bright spot here is that these teen-agers hold their views lightly, and there is ample evidence that they will firm their views (perhaps more positively toward business) during their formative years ahead.

The problem the professional manager and his corporation face in public acceptance is also born out by this recent experience. A group of business managers thought it might be helpful to discuss some of the current problems of society with representatives of other professions. At one such meeting, in this case with a group of ministers, the business manager were rather enthusiastic in presenting their philosophy, and in describing what they were doing to improve the total society environment.

One of the ministers obviously was becoming more and more puzzled as the discussion went along, and finally the chairman asked him – "It there something you don't understand?" The minister's reply was – "Yes, I am confused by the enthusiasm you have for business management. You seem to indicate you are interested in social welfare and in many things other than profit. I thought business management was the practice of exploiting labor simple to make a profit."

We, in private industry, have much to do to improve the image others have of us – but the image is less important than the performance. Management has accomplished quite a bit already, and it is going in the right direction.

Our philosophies are the same as yours. Our goals, by necessity, must be on a broader spectrum, but then collectively we are much larger. In dealing with the more all-encompassing segments of public welfare, we are not forgetting the individual private organizations such as yours that provide the day-by-day services that are so important to, and so thankfully received by, the people of this county. We will do all that we can to strengthen the public's realization of the significance of the role played by private charitable organization.

And, more important, the private business community will continue to help you and all of the other private charitable organizations in the task you have set for yourselves.

For our future in the American society, and for that matter, in the world society, is closely interwoven with yours.

Both are the essence of private initiative for the public good.

<u>*Chapter 9*</u>

Adapting to Social Changes

"Although it is dangerous to generalize, I would say that the student today more than anything else wants to become part of society; wants to cut through the hypocrisy that he sees all around him; and wants to get on with the problem of trying to solve what he feels are the social ills of the world. His inability to feel that he can make progress along these lines is at the root of many of today's student riots. He feels that the university structure is outmoded and that it is rigidly confining — that his voice of concern cannot be heard." [18]

Bill Hewlett

---

[18] "Acceptance Speech for Business Statesman of the Year," by Bill Hewlett, 4/13/70. (Courtesy of Agilent Technologies Inc. Archives)

William R. Hewlett Acceptance of Harvard Business School Club Award "Business Statesman of the Year" [19]

by
Bill Hewlett
(April 13th, 1970)

A great deal has been said and needs to be said about the increasing social responsibility of business. It has been pointed out that business management is only acting on the basis of enlightened self-interest when it expends time and effort in this area. I would like to feel that society is moving in a direction that allows the humanitarian component of every good manager to take an ever more active role as a constructive agent of social change.

I am not going to repeat the points that Walter Haas discussed on this occasion last year, but what I want to talk about is related.

I would like to talk about the young men and women that you will be hiring over the next few years and give you some personal views as to what I think they believe and want and

---

[19] "Acceptance Speech for Business Statesman of the Year," by Bill Hewlett, 4/13/70. (Courtesy of Agilent Technologies Inc. Archives)

what the business community might do about it. It has been said with some truth that whether we realize it or not, we are in the midst of a revolution as great as the Renaissance or the Industrial Revolution. The changes effected by this new revolution, and business' responses to them, have been extraordinarily profound and rapid.

As has been the case in the past, the university has been the focal point for thought as well as action. It is a mistake to think that the problems in our universities today are simply the result of acts of a handful of irresponsible radicals – not that those people are not present and involved. The radicals could not function at all if it were not for a very broad level of tacit support within the university community; not that the acts that the radicals perform are necessarily condoned as such, but rather that the average student sees in the radical a statement – albeit grossly exaggerated – of some of his own views on what should be done to direct society towards a better course. These convictions are quite deeply rooted in today's students. One can argue about how it happened, whose fault it was, etc., but the fact is that it is there and that we will shortly begin hiring these young people to work in our organizations.

What will be their reaction to the corporation and what will be the corporation's reaction to them? In this connection I think it should be realized that we are talking about an intellectual revolution. Perhaps this is best seen by the failure to date of the radical movement to penetrate the working community, or as it is often referred to, the "blue collar work force." Since it is an intellectual revolution, this means that the primary influence on management will be at the professional levels of employment.

Now the question may be asked, "Can there be a revolt in the corporation just as there was in the university?"

My answer is "Yes," but I have not the slightest idea of how, why, when or where.

Five years ago I doubt if there was one of you who could have predicted what has happened at Harvard, at Stanford, or at MIT, and yet we have seen deans thrown out of their offices at Harvard, the door of the president of MIT battered down, and red paint poured over the head of Stanford's president. It is well to draw a few lessons from the universities' experiences. It should be stated, however, that the average university today is more archaic than the corporation. In its authoritarian posture it is more like the corporation of the 19th Century. Human rights as they affect students are far less developed than in the outer world and governess in many cases is outmoded. Do not misunderstand me, corporations are far from perfect and universities are not all wrong, but there are basic differences between the university and the corporation.

Although it is dangerous to generalize, I would say that the student today more than anything else wants to become part of society; wants to cut through the hypocrisy that he sees all around him; and wants to get on with the problem of trying to solve what he feels are the social ills of the world. His inability to feel that he can make progress along these lines is at the root of many of today's student riots. He feels that the university structure is outmoded and that it is rigidly confining – that his voice of concern cannot be heard.

There is very little that I find I can agree with in William O. Douglas' "Points of Rebellion," but I do think that he catches their thoughts in his closing statements.

"The search of the youth today is more specific than the ancient search for the Holy Grail. The search of youth today is for ways and means to make the machine – and the vast bureaucracy of the corporation, state and of government that runs that machine – the servant of man."

These same young people will shortly be joining our organizations and bringing their views with them. They will be a group that is infinitely more idealistic than anything we have known in the past. I am sure that Dean Lawrence Fouracker will confirm my views on this point. They will readily join with the new theme of increased corporate social responsibility that is so evident today. They will also be questioning some of the most fundamental concepts on which the corporation is based – authority – responsibility – structure. In the field of corporate strategy they will be pushing more and more in the directions of programs that will lead to solutions to social problems rather than producing them. They will be asking for a corporate structure that is less rigid – this is more understanding of the individual. Incidentally, this is exactly what Robert Townsend is talking about in his book, "Up the Organization." In his humorous way he is criticizing many of the characteristics of the corporation that the younger generation find distasteful. Before this group I hesitate to mention Townsend's name, particularly after reading his section on the Harvard Business School, but feeling that you are basically broad-minded people, I thought I might get away with it.

These young people will be prone to question the "system" within the corporation. It will not suffice to say, "There does not have to be a reason, it's just policy." If you can't explain a regulation or a system, then the chances are that you don't really understand it yourself, or that it probably is not a valid regulation or system in the first place; but one thing is sure, you are not going to fool the ones that you most want to keep. Business is not like the military organization that operated on the basis of

"Theirs is not to make reply
Theirs is not to reason why,
Theirs is but to do or die."

This did not work in the colleges and it won't work (if it ever did) in business. The real authority will be the authority of knowledge and judgments and of leadership – not from the title on the door. All of this raises some very basic questions about what will be the relative responsibility on managers to their shareholders, to their employees, and to society at large.

(Parenthetically this is the issue now being raised by the Nader proxy statement in the General Motors matter.)

All of the above-cited influences will tend to place greater emphasis on responsibility to employees and society at large rather than on responsibility to shareholders. This will raise serious questions in the minds of the shareholders, for as a group, shareholders are probably the most reactionary or conservative component of the corporate structure. Yet it must be made clear to the shareholder what the cost-benefit ratios really are. He will have to be made to understand that in the long run these actions will cost him less – less in taxes – less in lack of efficiency – less in disruption to the economy. We have already come a long way since the time that corporate support to higher education was actively questioned by shareholders. Indeed, a very large corporation may more and more be considered a public trust rather than the private property of its shareholders. The company that can successfully adapt to such changing values will be at home and will represent a constructive force upon the changing society. The young men and women that you will be employing in the next few years can be the focal point that promotes and facilitates these changes. The companies that cannot adapt will find themselves out of step with the times – a relic of the past. These young people with their idealistic and sincere dedication, working in conjunction with the wisdom and understanding of an older generation and with the government that is sympathetic and helpful, can move us a long way toward solution to the complex problems facing us today.

When I chose the subject of these remarks, I had not read SRI's Long Range Planning Report on "Voices of Tomorrow." But when my draft was almost complete, I read this report and saw the accompanying film. I can do no better than to quote from the final pages of this report:

The candidate for a graduate degree in engineering economic systems was asked, "What, in your view, is the biggest mistake being made by business today?"

And his answer was, "If I were to put that in terms of just two words, I would say, "Not listening." Not listening in two ways: To the people who comprise the organization (the organization doesn't consist of plants and equipment, it consists of human beings, in the first instance"; not listening, then, within to the lower and middle echelon of its employees. And secondly, not listening to the forces outside, what we might call the hitherto voices in society such as those speaking out of the black community, out of the white radical student community who are forcing upon American society today a new set of values. They were the values which were brought in when this nation was first founded, framed in the Constitution. And what the youth and black people today are saying is that these radical views, radical for that time, are radical for this time, yet they can now be realized. The resources of society are sufficient that if we have the will, and we have the value system to do so, then they can be accomplished. And there is a great impatience worldwide, not just within this country, that this job be tackled, <u>now</u>."

Chapter 10

A Sad Day

"...There is little we can do to alleviate the nation-wide sorrow for the assassination of President Kennedy but to offer our prayers for him and his family — each in our individual way. .." [20]

Bill Hewlett

---

[20] "Memo to the employees," by Bill Hewlett, 11/63. (Courtesy of Agilent Technologies Inc. Archives)

Memo to the employees [21]

by
Bill Hewlett
(November 1963)

There is little we can do to alleviate the nation-wide sorrow for the assassination of President Kennedy but to offer our prayers for him and his family – each in our individual way. In this hour of tragedy for our country we should remember that the affairs of the world will and must go on. Since much of the work we do contributes directly to the strength and stature of our country we will carry on with our work today, but we urge any employees who wishes to attend a memorial service to take time off during the day to do so.

---

[21] "Memo to the employees," by Bill Hewlett, 11/63. (Courtesy of Agilent Technologies Inc. Archives)

Chapter 11

Too Much Inventory

"We finally reached the point, late in 1973, where it looked as though we were going to have to go out on the market for some long-term debt — something we had never done before. Since this was such a major departure from our "pay-as-you-go" policy at HP, I and some of the rest of our people got to thinking about the situation and we concluded that we had just botched up the job ourselves. We had failed to control assets, including inventory, in the way they should have been controlled. Because of the seriousness of the matter, I paid a visit to nearly every one of our divisions, worldwide, and gave them a lecture on the importance of controlling inventories and accounts receivable. I emphasized that they had to think about some things in addition to what was going on in their own department and divisions. I'll tell you, the response was impressive..." [22]

Dave Packard

---

[22] "Inventory Management and Control," by Dave Packard, 11/17/77. (Courtesy of Agilent Technologies Inc. Archives)

Inventory Management and Control [23]

by
David Packard

to
South Bay Chapter
Purchasing Management Association, Northern California
Palo Alto, California
(November 17th, 1977)

I am very pleased to be included in this program and to say a few words about the management of inventories, because this activity is a very important part of the overall management job. It is a complex subject, as I am sure you will conclude by the end of the evening, and it has a great many aspects. I'll try to cover at least a few of the more important aspects.

I will confine my remarks tonight to the management of inventories in a manufacturing industry. There are, of course, inventory management problems in the marketing industry and to a lesser extent the service industry – but I assume we want to direct our attention to the manufacturing industry.

To begin with, I think it would be useful to remind ourselves that there are three basic inventory categories in almost every

---

[23] "Inventory Management and Control," by Dave Packard, 11/17/77. (Courtesy of Agilent Technologies Inc. Archives)

manufacturing industry – the raw material or component side, the work-in-progress area, and the finished goods – and each of these has different problems. It is immediately apparent, therefore, that inventory concerns the purchasing manager, the manufacturing manager, and the marketing manager, and as a result you have a great many different inputs into inventory management/control. Thus, it is most important to keep in mind that the inventory management/control problem really must be considered as one part of overall asset management. Sometimes the people who have responsibility for a specific area, such as purchasing or manufacturing, may not appreciate that inventory management involves many other people in the organization.

It reminds me of the story about the merchant who was going to New York to purchase his Christmas stock; he was in fact acting as his own purchasing manager. He was working pretty hard to beat the prices down on everything he wanted to buy. He had taken his young son with him, and the young son observed all this. At the end of the day this fellow had done a pretty good job, he'd gotten the prices knocked down quite a bit on everything he'd ordered. When they left the shop, his son said, "Dad, why did you spend so much time beating these prices down when you know you probably won't be able to pay the bill?" His father said, "Well, son, you may be right. I may not be able to pay the bill. But I want you to know that this fellow is just the salt of the earth, he's one of my very good friends, and I wanted to minimize his losses."

Even as we look at the various details of the inventory control problem, and we <u>have</u> to look at details, it is very important that we keep the broader perspective in mind. Inventory, along with accounts receivable and cash or cash equivalents, makes up the current assets of a company. These are offset by accounts payable and by short-term notes. Together these items determine the working capital of the organization. Since no company, at least none that I have encountered yet, has unlimited resources, one of the overall aspects of inventory management is to minimize the working capital that is needed to support each dollar of sales. We must strive to do this, while at the same time taking actions, which will maximize the profits for each dollar of sales.

In the final analysis, particularly in a growth industry such as electronics, we have to generate a rate of return on assets, which is roughly equal to our sales growth rate. If we don't do this, things will get out of balance and we will find ourselves in a very difficult situation. The management of return on assets is an essential element in maintaining the viability of your company in the long term. Control of inventories is one of the variables, one of the ways you can have an impact on the control of assets – not only controlling the level, but also controlling the rate of return. A higher inventory is going to increase your costs and therefore tend to reduce your rate of return. Higher inventories, of course, require more capital, as well.

As this point, I'd like to take a few minutes to give you a case example which I think will point out the importance of managing inventories and what can be done when problems arise. It is a situation we experienced at our company over the past ten years, and I think the best way to approach this is to look at our level and growth rate of sales year-to-year, the corresponding growth of inventory in those years, and, most importantly, the percentage relationship between inventory and sales.

For many years we had been maintaining our total inventory in the range of 20 percent of our sales dollar – or a turnover of roughly five times a year if you want to put it in those terms. That was the situation in 1967 when we had sales of $245 million, and an inventory of $52 million, which represented 21 percent of sales. In 1968 sales grew 11 percent and inventory 12 percent, so we were retaining a reasonable balance, and our ratio of inventory to sales stayed at about 21 percent.

As we look on the situation now, it was in 1969 that we began to slip a little in our job of managing inventory. In that year our sales grew 19 percent to $324 million, while our inventories grew 33 percent to nearly $80 million. The following year sales increased 7 percent and inventories 11 percent. In 1971, it was 3 percent versus 6 percent, and the ratio of inventories to sales had risen to 24 percent. In 1972 sales rose 28 percent, inventories increased a little more than 30 percent, and the inventory/sales ratio had edged up to 25 percent.

In 1973 we had a substantial increase of 38 percent in sales, but inventories more than kept pace by increasing 59 percent. By that time inventories had grown to the point where they represented 29 percent of our annual sales volume, and we were faced with a very serious problem of financing this very large inventory build-up. The situation was compounded by the fact that we were experiencing a growth in accounts receivable, which is the other aspect of current assets.

Now, we were aware that these inventories were growing, and we had been reviewing the situation with our division managers year after year. I can assure you that we heard just about every excuse in the book for the situation. One we heard repeatedly was "Our business is changing, and we can't do this job right if our inventories don't go up."

We finally reached the point, late in 1973, where it looked as though we were going to have to go out on the market for some long-term debt – something we had never done before. Since this was such a major departure from our "pay-as-you-go" policy at HP, I and some of the rest of our people got to thinking about the situation and we concluded that we had just botched up the job ourselves. We had failed to control assets, including inventory, in the way they should have been controlled. Because of the seriousness of the matter, I paid a visit to nearly every one of our divisions, worldwide, and gave them a lecture on the importance of controlling inventories and accounts receivable. I emphasized that they had to think about some things in addition to what was going on in their own department and divisions. I'll tell you, the response was impressive.

We got the whole team working on the problem. We improved our planning. We regained better control of the detail of our inventories. We established, I think, a closer cooperation with our suppliers – a very important responsibility. We found that we could live with a smaller margin of safety. To give you just one specific, in the area of work-in-progress we had felt that we could save some money by putting sub-assemblies together in larger quantities and perhaps have a little more responsiveness in the final assembly stage. We discovered, however, that while we may have improved our costs to some extent, in some areas this practice had a serious impact on our total inventories.

At this point, I think it is worth mentioning that it is important to minimize the changes. There is nothing worse than starting in one direction and then altering your course. Again it gets back to planning and total commitment. No one single action will be effective in doing the job the way it ought to be done. No one person will be responsible.

Because of an outstanding effort by a very large number of people throughout the organization in 1974, our inventories increased by only 3 percent in comparison with a 34 percent increase in sales. This brought our inventory/sales ration down to 22 percent. A year later we were back to our traditional ratio of 21 percent, as sales increased 11 percent while inventories were held to a 5 percent increase. This kind of performance, I am glad to report, has continued through 1976 and 1977.

Now I recognize that this fairly dramatic turnaround probably caused some problems with a few of our suppliers. It caused some problems with some of our own people, because it has an effect on many of the things that were underway within the company. But I believe we resolved most of these problems to everyone's satisfaction.

One of the interesting figures I came up with as a result of thinking about what I might say tonight gives some indication of what would have happened to the company if we had not taken this action back in 1974. If the ration that existed between inventory and sales in 1973 still persisted today, it would have required $90 million more in inventory than we have at his particular time. That gives you some idea of the magnitude of the impact that this kind of overall control can have.

The message I want to get over this evening is that controlling inventories is a very important matter. If we had been smart enough, or wise enough, or energetic enough to have recognized this and done something about it back in the early 1970s, we would have saved our suppliers and our company some difficulty. The responsibility of inventory control goes beyond individual problems. It is not the isolated job of one person, or one department. It extends into almost every aspect of your organization, and it involves almost everyone – purchasing, manufacturing, and marketing.   The marketing people, for example, have to realize that they can't always have the inventory of finished goods they'd like for immediate delivery, and they have to recognize that good planning is essential.

Now, we've been talking about the problems in the internal management aspects of inventory control, but I'm sure you all recognize that there are some external factors, which just make the situation even more complex. One of these factors is that we are operating in an environment of very high utilization of capacity by suppliers; it makes the flow of components and materials more difficult to control. Hence, it encourages such things as double-ordering (which is not really beneficial to anyone in the long run) and larger inventories that might be avoidable otherwise.

Inflation also is a problem, as you know. Most of the thinking in our company about inventories was developed and then carried forward from the period of the fifties and sixties when inflation was not a significant problem. When it got into double-digit inflation a couple of years ago, we didn't recognize it but there is one aspect here that is very important. It brought about re-thinking of the "last in-first out" handling of inventory costs. I remember going to Brazil some time in the late sixties, and attending a luncheon with a group of people there. At the time the annual inflation rate in Brazil was something in excess of 100 percent per year. "How do you deal with this kind of situation?" I asked one of the men attending the luncheon. "Well", he said, "it's very simple. If you are in the merchandising business you buy your Christmas inventories in January the year ahead for Christmas. If you do that you're in pretty good shape." So, sometimes these external influences will encourage you to do things that you wouldn't possibly think about doing otherwise.

That brings me to the final point I want to make. Inventory control is a complex and important job but it simply cannot be done by formula or by computer procedure. Computer procedures will help you, and in fact there are many aids available to you in planning and measuring your appropriate levels and in determining where you are. But, if the job of managing inventories is going to be done the way it should be done, it's going to require imagination and hard work and dedication on all levels. The final objective, for anyone who has anything to do with inventories, has to be to take every step possible to keep the profits up and the inventories down. It's just as simple as that.

<u>*Chapter 12*</u>

Managing in Tough Times

"...And so it is consistent with this policy of considering the company as a team that when times are difficult, we don't take it out on the lowest man on the totem pole..." [24]

Bill Hewlett

---

[24] "Tape Transcription of Remarks by President Bill Hewlett, Meeting of Managers and Supervisors," by Bill Hewlett, 7/1/70. (Courtesy of Agilent Technologies Inc. Archives)

Tape Transcription of Remarks by President Bill Hewlett, Meeting of Managers and Supervisors [25]

by
Bill Hewlett
Palo Alto, California
(July 1st, 1970)

I know that there have been many rumors around the plant having to do with what we are going to do with our work week and I think we ought to start out by saying that we are going to have to reduce the work week every fortnight. By that I mean that we will work four days one week and five days the next. Now, having gotten that out on the table let me talk about some of the background of this and about how it will operate.

As you know, I have tried to indicate this in the articles in Measure that the U.S. economy is not particularly booming at this point and that we have been partially sustained by our foreign business. The fact of the matter is that the incoming order rate, be it domestic or foreign, simply has not been able to keep up with our ability to produce. The result is we have seen an erosion of our backlog and an increase in our inventory. Just to give you an idea of the magnitude of this – in just the last twelve months our inventory has increased $23 million. It has

---

[25] "Tape Transcription of Remarks by President Bill Hewlett, Meeting of Managers and Supervisors," by Bill Hewlett, 7/1/70. (Courtesy of Agilent Technologies Inc. Archives)

almost increased by one-third in that twelve-month period. I would like to point out that our policy of trying to maintain a very low debt has been held for exactly this reason. Because this very low debt has allowed us to increase our inventory by this amount, and not adversely affect our ability to borrow money for our operation. We are still able to borrow on commercial paper at practically a prime rate, I guess you'd say, Van, and without having to pay the penalties that many companies do for not having as clean a balance sheet.

I suppose the first question comes as to why one day in ten off. It simply turns out that this is a pretty fair approximation of the difference between our ability to produce with our present staff and our rate of incoming orders. There are a number of ways that this could be approached – the traditional way is simply to lay-off 10 percent of your people. On the other hand, this I don't feel is a very equitable way, and certainly it is not in the tradition under which HP has operated for many years. As you know, the bonus plan itself recognizes that all people are considered as equal participants in the success of the corporation. And that the janitor gets exactly the same percentage increase due to profit sharing and retirement that I do, or anyone else in the company. And so it is consistent with this policy of considering the company as a team that when times are difficult, we don't take it out on the lowest man on the totem pole. Now, this is not a traditional approach and I am not concerned by the lack of tradition. I think that it is an equitable way and a way that each one of our employees can understand – although, obviously, it will be difficult for a number of our people, and I will talk about that a little bit later.

There were several ways, of course, that having decided that we would slow down the clock, that this might have been done. We might have worked, let's say, seven hours a day rather than eight – or we might have worked four and one-half days a week – or we might have worked as I suggest four days one week and five days the next. After considering all the pros and cons, it seemed that the latter approach was by far the fairest. If one takes, let's say as an example an engineer who is not a clock-puncher, if we merely said that he was expected to work seven hours rather than eight hours, you know very well that he would still work eight hours, and I can say this for an awful lot of other people. Similarly, if we had gone to a four and one-half hour week, we would have a similar situation – let's say the half-day was on Friday, for many of you would have the same results and it would have broken up a day. By providing it all in one time, it seems that it would have the least detrimental impact to all of you. And after all, this is summer time and if you do have to have eight hours off, it would probably seem better to be able to take it off at one time in conjunction with the weekend. If this had been winter, perhaps for some of you who don't ski, it wouldn't have been as good a decision.

Let me talk specifically about what we are trying to do. We will work four days one week and work five days the next. Starting the first day off will be the Friday of next week, which would be the 10th of July.

The next logical question – how long will it last. Well, obviously it depends on the state of the economy and what happens to our order level. But I am not planning on this thing lasting beyond the end of this fiscal year, which means four months. By that time, the normal attrition that we have that is about one percent per month, and a continued judicial evaluation of some of our marginal employees, should bring the employment level down to an appropriate level if the economy does not improve by the beginning of the fiscal year.

Who is affected by this plan? Basically, all of our domestic operations, our plants, our overhead, our officers, managers, engineers, except the following operations: Avondale, because Avondale has already had very heavy layoffs and their order rate is now very much in line with their ability to produce; Colorado Springs...Colorado Springs is in a similar position, they have a substantial backlog and their current rate of incoming orders is excess of their ability to produce; San Diego...San Diego is roughly in balance, but face a difficult move starting in August, in which they will have to replace a number of people, and it seems inappropriate to be knocking off two days of work and then asking the people to be working overtime the next month; and the Automatic Measurements Division... this is the one that is working on the systems like the Swedish Air Force and the F-111. They have over twelve months backlog and are working night and day to try to get this equipment out, and it would be absolutely inexcusable to say that they had to take off two days a month.

There will obviously be a few special cases where given operations are having to work overtime and they cannot transfer people into it because you are machine-limited. There is an example of a small group of about five people at HPA trying to make pilot lights, and they are behind and they have to keep going.

We will make special arrangements with our field engineers because they are on a fundamentally different method of compensation and you can't simply tell a field engineer that he works 10 percent less. We will have to make other adjustments.

Fundamentally, I want to point out that this is a slowdown of 10 percent and not basically an effort to reduce costs. Obviously, the slowdown will result in reduced costs, but I want to point out that because it is a slowdown of the clock it is worth looking at what happens to our benefits programs. There is some problem in life insurance because there are certain people that will swing from week to week because they are at a break point in the life insurance cut-off and this represents kind of a tough problem – I guess, Betty, for your computer – but fundamentally we will be able to solve this. Items such as group medical hospital insurance, vacations, sick leave, cash profit-sharing, preferred profit-sharing, stock purchase, will all be subject to the same regulations as they were before. Except where they are wage-related, they will be reduced by the appropriate 10 percent factor.

The question also comes up with reference to new hires. Obviously, at a time that we are reducing our effective workweek, we are not anxious to take on new hires. On the other hand, there are certain forward commitments that we have made, particularly in the field of engineering, and we will advise these people that the job is still here, but that in the interim they will be working at a rate that is 10 percent less than the amount agreed upon. Obviously, we will try to kill all overtime, although there may be a few special cases in which we will have to have overtime. Our summer help program is an important program and I do not propose to change this. They are just as much employees of this company as anyone else, and they will therefore take the 10 percent cut, but they will not be discriminated against.

We will obviously try and pull in all the subcontracting that we can where our equipment allows us to do it. We have certain part-time employees that traditionally have worked part-time for us. We will continue to employ these people because, again, they are HP employees, but for particular reasons they are not working full-time.

As I mentioned earlier, this is not fundamentally a program to try and cut expenses. It is a program to try and make our production match our order rate. Thus, there is no need for such items as talking about cutting off the picnic or cutting off coffee and doughnuts, and things like this, because this is not basically the problem. Basically, the problem is to get our production in live with our order picture.

As far as capital expenditures are concerned, we have tried to push off or defer all the capital expenditures that we can. And we are now proposing a rate of capital expenditure that is about 15 percent less than we planned from the beginning of the year. You may ask why do we continue with Building 6 and why do we continue with fitting out the Granger Building. Obviously, Building 6 is under contract – it would probably cost us more to terminate that contract than it would to finish it up and furthermore, I consider this a temporary situation and I look for a return to more happy days probably some time in the middle of '71.

If we had to do it over again, I don't think we would have acquired the lease on the Granger Building. But the fact of the matter is that we did, and we have plans under way and it simply turns out that it is virtually impossible to turn off some of these plans, although we will try and keep to a minimum the expenditures at Granger.

Obviously, as far as the public is concerned, they should not be particularly conscious of the fact that we have chosen to not work one day each fortnight. By that I mean that this will not be announced to the public. But if someone calls up on a Friday, they have the right to expect someone to answer the phone and answer some of their questions. Thus, there must be some facilities that are manned even on these Fridays off. We will have to do this by means of rotation. So as an example in my office, probably on one Friday Madie will be off and on the other Friday Kathy will be off. This is going to take considerable juggling and I am not saying this is going to be a smooth operation, but we do have to maintain a position to the public.

It is obviously true with reference to the fields of effective marketing people and in the factories. If people call in about problems there has to be someone there to answer them.

It is important to point out that these days off cannot be counted as days of paid vacation. Let me just put this in a very good example. We are talking about thirteen days, plus or minus, to the end of the fiscal year. Let's just say that we took all our vacations together and they represented thirteen days. You really haven't achieved anything because you have the same work force working the same total number of hours, and we haven't solved our problem. Thus, we cannot consider these days off as days of paid vacation. They must be in addition to the paid vacation days.

Let me just touch on a few points as to the effect of this to the extent that we can foresee it. Basically, as I mentioned with a few exceptions, base pay will be reduced by 10 percent. This will amount to a savings or a lack of expenditure if you wish, of about $900,000 a month. Because we will be continuing our profit-sharing and retirement plans on the same basis as we have in the past, basically this money will appear on the bottom right-hand of the page and will be subject to the 22 percent that is represented by profit-sharing and preferred retirement, which really in terms of total payroll is about 12 percent of payroll. So the pay cut will not really be at 10 percent, it will be closer to 8.8 percent. Now I assure you that this was not planned this way but it is fortunate that this action coincides exactly with the taking off of the surtax on the Federal income tax, which occurs on 1 July. I think it might be helpful to cite a couple of cases of what this means. For a married person with no dependents, this will mean that he will receive a 4 ½ percent increase in his take-home pay – so that this in part litigates against this 8.8 percent. On the other hand, someone that has five dependents that I once had and let's say who is making $1200 a month, as I might observe I once made, this will represent a 7 percent increase, and for a person who is making $700 a month this will represent a 9 percent increase. Thus, somewhere between the figures you can find yourself and you can see that there will be considerable softening of this in terms of what this really means to you in terms of take home pay. In addition, the Social Security which represents 4.8 percent and is paid on the first $7800 of pay, for some of you will be coming off about this time, it will be exactly for those of you who make $1300 a month, this will come off on 1 July and actually, knowing your own salary, you can figure out whey you will cease paying this.

I realize that there are going to be cases in which this is going to be difficult for individuals and I don't know of any way that we can have prevented that. I can assure you that laying people off 100 percent is a lot harder on people than it is trying to spread this out over a broader base.

In summation, I think this is the only fair way. I am not concerned about the long-term health of the company. We have a good team and it is exactly for this reason I don't want to lose people. Now this is a very complex question and one of the reasons we have as many of you here is to not only allow you to go back to your foremen and talk with them, because at 11:00 a.m. I will make an announcement to the plant at large and you need to be there to answer questions of your people, but also because I am sure that amongst you here there are a lot of very practical question that have come to mind and I have a team of experts down here in the front row that guarantee they are going to answer any of these questions that you care to ask – at least I have tried to have them consider as many of these as they could. So I would like to answer what questions you may have. Yes.

Question: How strongly should I discourage people from coming in on the second Friday?

Answer: I think that we really want to consider this a plant shut-down on that particular Friday with the exception of these swing people. Now if there are conscientious people who do want to come in, I don't think we've got a right to say they can't. But I think we want to make it very clear that we certainly don't expect them to come in and we should try and discourage them from doing it. I think it is unfair to these people who are indeed conscientious.

Question: Will the reduction result uniformly in a 10% pay reduction?

Answer: I don't know, Ray. For the hourly workers it is easy. For the salaried workers, I would think that it would be just simpler to level it out and say that it is 10 percent and that salaried people reduce it 10 percent. Does that close out your thinking right?

Question ?

Answer: Okay. Yeah, I'm right.

Question: Kirby –

Answer: I didn't say it wouldn't be announced to the public, but that the public would not be conscious of it – there is a slight difference. That's not a remark against your department, Kirby. We are required by our agreement with the Stock Exchange that any material changes in the corporation be announced to the Stock Exchange. Therefore, we will be issuing a news release to the Exchange, but obviously we are not going to be calling up all of the newspapers in the United States and telling them that we are reducing our workweek. What I was trying to say in the other respect was that as far as our customers are concerned, they have the right to expect that people will be here to answer their questions where possible. Other questions? Yes.

Question: When and on what criteria will the decision be reviewed?

Answer: This is a firm decision as far as the month of July is concerned. Each month thereafter, we will review the various operating units and decide whether their order level is sufficient to warrant them returning toward a fuller workweek. This will continue to be reviewed month-by-month, but there will be no reviews in July – we have already made the July review. Yes.

Question: Isn't this action likely to bring about union organization activity?

Answer: As always, I think the question of labor unions rests as much as anybody on the first and second line of supervisors and their ability to interpret what the company does and means. I think that most people who would be subject to labor union influences also understand the economic situation and they can look around and see their brethren being laid off in other areas. I think if this is presented to them carefully, and reasons are made clear, particularly if it is pointed out that the fortunate effect of the tax change is going to soften this blow considerably, that we will probably not have much trouble as you might anticipate. Let me just take another number from my curve. Let's just say that the average employee that you are talking about is married, has two dependents and he is making somewhere between $700-$900 a month. His tax forgiveness is going to be 6 percent and so the net effect of this is only 2.8 percent, which really is not too bad. I might point out that it is more favorable to the lower paid employee than it is to the higher paid employee because the effects of the change in dependents allowance will represent a larger percentage of his salary than it does for the higher paid people.

Question: It think it is worth noting that the effect is greatly lessened when averaged over the full year.

Answer: That is a good point, too. If you look at the annual wage through the year, this represents really 3 percent.

Question: Where people have really locked themselves in, in anticipation of continuing good times, have any provisions been made to help them?

Answer: No, there has not, but if there are really, really tough cases we will be glad to deal with them individually as we always have.

Question: If a day off occurs during a paid vacation, should he be paid or not?

Answer: Now I anticipated that question and I asked someone down here to be able to answer it. Who can answer it? To simplify the question, and I guess it would be a paraphrase, "Supposing a guy is in the middle of his vacation and this unpaid work day occurs during the middle of his vacation, as an example, how is this treated? Who can answer that? The total accrued vacation does not change.

Question: Could you tell us again how you came up with 8.8 percent out of 10 percent?

Answer: I thought that was rather nicely done myself. These savings that will accrue by not working will come out of dollars not paid. They, therefore, appear at the bottom right hand side of the profit and loss statement. Therefore, they are subject to profit sharing and deferred retirement. Now, if you look at profit sharing as deferred retirement, on an average they represent 12 percent of base payroll. So, the employees that will be taking a 10 percent cut in pay, but they will be receiving 1.2 percent more in their profit-sharing because of this. Now it doesn't mean that they are really going to receive more, but receive more compared to if we had not take these days off...And if they are in the plan, right. Thank you.

Question: What about (missed on tape)

Answer: This is just one of the 101 details that we are going to have to work out.

Question: Will the cutback have an adverse effect on our profits?

Answer: No, it will actually have a favorable effect on our profit margin, because the assumption is that we are going to be producing the same amount of goods. There is no point in producing goods and putting them into the inventory, and we have been chewing down our backlog to the point that we no longer have a safe backlog to operate on. So that we would have had to reduce our production by 10 percent.

Question: Isn't the basic problem one of reducing costs?

Answer: Let me just propose two solutions to this problem and you will see, I think, what the difference is. Supposing we just cut everybody's pay 10 percent, which doesn't seem to work. We would have had a cost reduction of 10 percent, but we would not have solved our basic problem. The basic problem is that we are producing faster than our orders are coming in. So what we have to do is reduce our production by 10 percent to make it fit the order rate. So we have got to stop producing equipment by about 10 percent. That means that if everyone works just 90 percent of what they did before and are paid for 90 percent, but we produce the only amount that we can ship, and that is our orders, then indeed compared to just producing willy nilly, we have cut payroll expenses by this 10% factor which is about $900,000 a month. So it is a question of where the emphasis is.

I might point out that this inventory now has gone up $23 million and is now at $77 million, and if you figure that our money is costing us 10 percent, that is $7.7 million a year, roughly in interest charges. Now, we have not borrowed that amount, but the point is that an incremental basis is a valid statement.

Question: ??

Answer: That is interesting.   Betty says that $77 million is
within $1 million of our base payroll for a year. Excuse me, I'm
sorry, it's $87 million – it was $77 million at the beginning of
the year and $87 million now.

Question: What about someone earning only $500 a month?

Answer: Well, the only curve I have is 700 and I guess that is
not going to affect it too much. What number of dependents
do you want? ...I don't know what an average dependent is, but
all I can say is I have three points on the curve -- $700, $900
and $1200 per month, and for two dependents at $700 per
month it is 6 percent; and $700 and $90 are right on top of each
other and therefore I assume probably $500 would be the same
point.

Question: Why should R&D people not work 100 percent?

Answer: Well, that question came up before and, number one,
for the R&D people there are a lot of facilities R&D people will
need that will not be available on that day. The second thing is,
that if I were back in R&D and I offered the choice of being
paid the same amount of money and having a Friday off or not
having a Friday off, I think I would rather take the Friday
off...Yeah, but that's kind of set by the calendar, isn't it? I
think the answer is that there are all shades of gray in this thing
and once you start making special cases, there is no end to

where you go and I just can't bleed for the poor engineer who has the choice of working ten days or nine days and we are asking him to work nine instead of ten and paying him the same amount.

Question: ??

Answer: They are.

Question: How do you decide when a division is over producing?

Answer: Well, how long do you think we ought to produce for inventory? How long do you think we ought to cut into our backlog? What point do you think is enough? That is the point I am trying to make that this is not primarily a problem of trying to increase our profits, it is a problem of trying to get our production and our orders in line...We did do it selectively. We took the plants that had orders to match their production capability and those people remaining up and those plants that are down on their orders, and the overhead people we're pulling down. You know, this is a no win game. No one likes it. You try and come up with what represents the most equitable possible solution and you know, if we planned for this thing for a year, maybe we would have had a slight different program. But I really think this is about as close to an equitable base as you can get.

Question: ??

Answer: No, I don't really have any pointers for this. As I indicated earlier, I think attrition is going to help to some extent to get our employment down. I think that selective evaluation of marginal employees should continue, and between those two, I would hope that by the start of the fiscal year and with a slight upturn we may be able to return to a full workweek.

Question: ??

Answer: No, that is what I said. On a monthly basis, we will review division by division.

Question: ??

Answer: I think it does. I think there are so few of them we have to look at them individually and see what they are doing, but by in large, I would say yes. Well, I think that probably covers most of the questions and if you have any further questions before you go back to your employees, you can probably get in touch with your division or group managers.

Carl Cottrell asked the Data Products people to come back because apparently they don't understand these things very well and he has got to explain it to them. Thank you very much.

<u>*Chapter 13*</u>

Maximizing Corporate Resources

"...Setting the objectives does not finish the job. People must be encouraged to innovate, and unless new ideas can be somehow brought forth, the job will be poorly done or not at all. Here freedom and motivation are important. Management cannot innovate a new product – the individuals working on the job must do so. They must be left free to do it their way. But their motivation comes largely from recognition. The important thing is that every new product project is a total company responsibility. " [26]

Dave Packard

---

[26] "Making Maximum Utilization of Corporate Resources," by Dave Packard, 9/19/63. (Courtesy of Agilent Technologies Inc. Archives)

Making Maximum Utilization of Corporate Resources [27]

by
Dave Packard
(September 19th, 1963)

Today we are living in a rapidly changing world, a world changing under the impact of science and the advancement of knowledge. From the atom we have an unlimited source of energy to add to that of the fossil fuels, which spawned the industrial revolution two centuries ago. Within three decades we have increased the speed of travel from a few hundred miles per hour to eighteen thousand miles per hour. We can do in a matter of minutes computations which two decades ago would have required many man years. This breath-taking progress in man's ability to master his environment has achieved more in our lifetime than has been achieved since the beginning of civilization and the pace of this progress is increasing.

It is not unreasonable to expect that such momentous advances in man's mastery of his environment would also vastly accelerate changes in man's relationship with his fellow man. And there are great social changes underway. Social changes move more slowly and so it is too early to determine clearly the nature, magnitude, or significance of these social changes, but there is ample evidence they are taking place. They stem from

---

[27] "Making Maximum Utilization of Corporate Resources," by Dave Packard, 9/19/63. (Courtesy of Agilent Technologies Inc. Archives)

greatly expanded communication, the radio, television, the press – they are nurtured by a rapid increase in literacy and understanding. These social changes are the inevitable result of, and at the same time catalog, a rising level of education of all people.

We see on every side a fervent of dissatisfaction with things the way they are. There is a rising tide of hope everywhere for a better life because it now seems possible of realization. We see it most strikingly in the underdeveloped countries, but we find it here too in the United States among our minority and under-privileged groups of people. It even extends into discussions of problems in the local community.

Just as the job and responsibility of management is under the influence of science and the material changes which result, the job and responsibility of management is under the influence of the social changes which are taking place today. While the direction and extent of the social change taking place cannot yet be determined, there are clearly some effects which are important to management people. The most obvious is the fact that more people are obtaining more education at every level in society. More people can read and write and understand. The frontiers of knowledge are advancing very rapidly and many people are being educated right up to these frontiers. Here, then, is a resource growing in magnitude and in value and it must not be overlooked. The changing social patterns are also having a profound influence on markets for industry. Changes in consumer buying patterns in the industrialized countries are providing an insatiable demand for new products of all kinds and particularly for more sophisticated products – home appliances and recreational equipment, for example. But the rising aspirations of people in underdeveloped countries are generating tremendous markets for the essentials – food, housing, clothing and transportation. And these expanding markets which are part and parcel of today's social flux are by no means unimportant to those of us in management.

From the great scientific developments of the past few decades, we have inherited a vast array of resources to apply to the management job. We have unlimited energy for our factories. We have automation to control our machines. We have communication facilities to transmit any amount of information we require. We have sophisticated instruments and procedures to collect our data and we have computers to process it for us. And as we expand this list of physical resources we have the ability to make almost any product, even a vehicle to go to the moon. But the all important question remains – how do we effectively utilize these resources we have at our command?

Sometimes as one reviews these many resources, which are available to management, one is tempted to toy with the idea that the whole affair might be made completely impersonal. Not just the factory, but the entire business might be automated. But this fantasy is soon dismissed when one remembers that machines cannot yet think or innovate, and probably never will. And if you will accept that premise, at least for now, you inevitably come to the conclusion that the ability to think, to innovate, is now vastly more important than it ever was, simply because these vast impersonal resources must be effectively utilized.

Now the traditional resources, which the corporate manager had to utilize, were money, raw materials, energy and human labor – the latter largely as a source of energy. Much of the theory of management was about how to utilize these traditional resources efficiently.

Financial techniques were developed to determine how well the manager used the money he had available. These included measures of profit on sales, return on investment, current ration, ratios of equity vs. borrowed capital, and so on.

Methods were also developed to determine how efficiently the manager utilized his raw materials. Depletion controls for mineral resources were so important in some industries that they have become integrated into our tax laws. Businesses have risen and fallen on their ability to command and control sources of raw materials.

And the beginning of scientific management came from how to utilize human labor more effectively. Many of the things we still talk about in management are how to get a bit more work out of our people. Time and motion studies were designed to show the worker how he could use his physical capability more effectively. Piece work recognized the proposition that if you gave the worker an incentive, he might be able to figure out how to do his job better than you as a manager could tell him or show him. This was an important recognition of the fact that an employee might contribute something more than physical labor if you gave him a chance.

The trend of management thinking, particularly over the past decade or two, has been directed more and more toward the management of the human resources of an organization. The fact that we have a rapidly expanding impersonal scientific base for our affairs places more importance on people rather than less. And fortunately we have the kind of people we need in increasing numbers to do this job well.

I would propose then that the efficient utilization of people, as our most important corporate resource, is the sum and substance of management today. The value of people is primarily in their ability to think, to innovate, to bring imagination rather than their physical energy to their jobs. There are many ways in which people can be encouraged to apply their intelligence to their jobs and this can and should be done in every area of a business. Today I want to discuss how this can be done in two specific areas: the utilization of the resource generally described as "know-how" in a day-to-day manufacturing operation, and the capability of an organization to develop new products considered as an important corporate resource. Both depend on the effective utilization of people rather than money or physical assets.

With the vast amount of published material on every conceivable subject – books, technical magazines, published papers by specialists in every field of endeavor – one might think that all the "know-how" necessary for efficient corporate operation would be available for the asking. But our experience tells us there is a decisive difference between reading how to do something and being able to do it. Experience – the ability to make the idea actually work – is the priceless ingredient the expert person brings to the job. The more complicated the problem, the more necessary the expert person becomes.

As I walk through one of our manufacturing plants, I am always amazed at the hundreds of extremely complicated jobs which are accomplished with apparent ease. Behind each of these jobs is the work of an expert, a specialist who has taken advantage of the knowledge available to him, reduced it to practice, often by experimentation or long hours of careful work. I recall many cases where we were unsuccessful in a particular job until we found the right man to work it out. Some people have the ability to innovate, while some do not. Even a few people with such an ability is a very important resource to develop, and every successful company has a great store of special know-how – a great asset which provides an advantage for the organization. But at the same time I have never seen an organization, which would not benefit from more special know-how. There are always innumerable problems to be solved. There are always jobs, which should be done better.

What, then, is the method of developing and utilizing this important resource? Unique and valuable know-how comes from people who are able to innovate. Such people can be identified by trial and error – perhaps in other ways, too, although I do not know of any. They operate best in an environment of freedom. They are professionals in the true sense, not managers or organization men. Management has not always recognized the importance of this ability to innovate, and when present, it is often stifled by restraints and controls. With the growing complexity, particularly of a technologically oriented business, people who have the ability and opportunity to innovate are a great resource, which must be effectively utilized.

The people who are most effective at innovation often do not fit into the normal organizational pattern. They are usually not good executives or administrators. One way they can be utilized is as specialists in a given functional area. Give this type of person a special problem area to work on and then let him have the freedom to do it his way.

Since every operation group, particularly in a large corporation, develops a certain amount of its own know-how – and this should be encouraged – how can the specialist make his contribution? The answer is very simple and pragmatic. If the specialist is the right man, the operating group will seek out and use his help – his is the authority of knowledge. His motivation and satisfaction come largely from his being able to see his know-how put to practical use.

The precise way in which this important resource of innovation by individuals is utilized on the day-to-day problems of a corporation can vary widely. The first step is to recognize that people can contribute by innovation. They must be given some general guidance, which should restrict them as little as possible. It should be a general objective – reduction of cost on a particular job, improvement of quality on a product, or the development of a process on which a new product depends.

The second step is to give the people who can do this kind of work some operating freedom. You have to tell them or give them guidance as to what you want done. Then you have to let them do it their way.

The third step is to make sure the people who make contributions by innovation in your organization receive credit for what they do. They are much more likely to do a good job the next time if they receive some recognition for the last one.

We have in our company a number of such specialists. They provide a great deal of invaluable know-how in all areas of the company. They have developed for us manufacturing techniques, which lower our costs and improve our quality. Their innovations have, over the years, been one of our most important sources of profitability. Their contributions have been recognized through out the company. We consider one of our most important management challenges that of expanding their influence and developing their opportunities to innovate.

A second and most important resource of our company has been our capability to develop and market new products. This capability also comes, of course, from individuals who are able to innovate. But there must also be guidance and direction if this effort is to be efficient. Innovation in the field of day-to-day know-how is well directed because there is a specific job to be done, or a problem to be solved, and the expert is readily directed to the problem. There is almost no limit to the variety of new products, which might be developed. With limited resources in money and people, the all-important question is which project is most significant? What is the priority among all possible projects?

Studies have indicated that of all the new product projects initiated by industry, only a very small percentage is ultimately successful. Thus, while more successful new products would probably result from an increase in total new product development effort, there appears to be considerable room for improvement in the results, which can be achieved with the present level of effort.

Yet many successful companies achieve excellent success from their research and development expenditure. Crawford Greenewalt, reporting as board chairman of the DuPont Company, stated that for every dollar they spend in the laboratories on research and development, they have sooner or later spent three dollars for new plants and processes to produce the products they have developed. And the growth and profitability of DuPont is a magnificent tribute to the efficiency and success of their new product program.

The growth, and I believe the profitability of our company, is the direct result of our new product effort, and so a word about our program may be of interest.

Our sales in 1962 were $109,000,000 over half of which came from new products developed since 1957. On a corporate-wide basis, for every dollar spent on new product development, five dollars in profits before taxes have been generated, and in addition, the dollar spent on research and development has been recovered.

Without question the most important step in a new product program is the initial selection of the project to be undertaken. No company has unlimited resources in either money or manpower, and it is mandatory that the resources available be applied to the projects most likely to be successful. Toward this end certain guiding policies have been adopted, and a specific procedure has been followed.

Since the character of a company tomorrow is determined by the product it is developing today, and since we intend to remain exclusively in the field of electronic instrumentation, all new product projects are limited to this field. We often encounter new ideas in our laboratories, which could be the basis of other products, but since our manufacturing, and marketing capabilities are directed toward instrumentation, we limit our new product development to this field. One would think such a policy would be obvious, but many concerned fail to coordinate their new product programs with rational overall corporate objectives, and end up with good products but no manufacturing or marketing capability to exploit the products.

We have found from experience that the new product with the largest measure of innovation are most successful. In other words, when a competitor is well established in a market – even a very attractive market – it is difficult to achieve a satisfactory market position unless the new product is in itself an important contribution to the art of measurement.

These guidelines stem from overall corporate policy and provide broad objectives, which each new product project must meet. The proposed product must be in the field of electronic instrumentation, and it must, if possible, bring some new contribution to the field – not be just a copy of something someone else has already done. But in addition to these general objectives, we need to provide specific guidance for the project.

Each new product is carefully investigated by marketing and manufacturing people before it is approved. Often exploratory research in the laboratory is necessary to evaluate the technical feasibility of the idea, but before substantial resources are committed, a well-defined procedure is followed.

First, the marketing and the technical people, working together, prepare a tentative specification for the proposed product.

Usually the proposed product is discussed with potential customers for their reaction. The marketing people then prepare a five-year forecast of sales volume. From this an estimate of five years' profit is made. The research and development people prepare a time schedule for the development and estimate the cost – including production engineering and estimated development cost then becomes a figure of merit for that project. With a figure of merit thus calculated for each proposed project, we have a fair method of comparing projects and selecting the most attractive for development. The detailed specifications of the proposed project and the figure of merit calculations provide a very specific objective for the project. These provide guidance toward what the product will be, what it will cost, what will be the volume, and what will be the resulting profit. These specific objectives are kept before the development team throughout the course of development.

Setting the objectives does not finish the job. People must be encouraged to innovate, and unless new ideas can be somehow brought forth, the job will be poorly done or not at all. Here freedom and motivation are important. Management cannot innovate a new product – the individuals working on the job must do so. They must be left free to do it their way. But their motivation comes largely from recognition. The important thing is that every new product project is a total company responsibility. Marketing people, manufacturing people, financial people, as well as the development engineers, are continually involved from the beginning and work together.

This procedure provides not only a useful method of evaluations and decision making at the beginning but also continual communication between interested people during the entire development process. It provides strong motivation for the innovation.

The people who are responsible for innovation – the development people – are in continual contact with the manufacturing and marketing people. The project engineer thus receives company-wide recognition if his product is successful. He is encouraged to help introduce his new product in the field as well. He thereby receives much more satisfaction and motivation from accomplishment than if he was involved only in the laboratory technical development.

These two illustrations of contributions by people working as individuals, or as part of a team are only examples of the many ways in which human resources can be effectively utilized. The requirements for effective encouragement of individual resourcefulness are actually very simple. The first is to provide for a common objective. This objective may be a level of profit performance, it may be a target for cost reduction, or it may be a new product with a carefully defined and extensive set of objectives.

Motivation comes from many things, but one of the best methods of motivation is recognition. In recognition of an individual contribution, both freedom and motivation are encouraged, and both are key elements to encourage the individual to contribute his ability.

In simple form then, one very useful approach to the better utilization of human resources in management is: Provide a well-defined objective, give the person as much freedom as possible in working toward that objective, and finally, provide motivation by seeing that the contribution of the individual is recognized throughout the organization. This is an attitude that can be applied in many ways, but when applied will help assure the maximum utilization of the most important corporate resource of all – the individual capability of all of our people.

<u>*Chapter 14*</u>

On Foreign
Competition

"We have no trouble in telling our purchasing people that, given all the facts involved, we ought to lean a little bit toward buying products from our American supplier, and I would hope that everybody else does likewise." [28]

Dave Packard

---

[28] "Encroachment of Japanese Firms on Today's Semiconductor and Tomorrow's Electronic and Computer Industries," by Dave Packard, 11/16/78. (Courtesy of Agilent Technologies Inc. Archives)

Encroachment of Japanese Firms on Today's Semiconductor and Tomorrow's Electronics and Computer Industries [29]

By
David Packard

Excerpts from Dave's speech for the following: South Bay Chapter of The Purchasing Management Association, November 16, 1978…."Top Management Night"

Last year at this corresponding meeting I wrote up a very carefully prepared speech, and it turned out that everyone had said everything that I was going to say. This time I decided not to prepare anything, but rather to make some comments on what the other speakers have said. I am sure that you agree with me that there have been a great many interesting and stimulating ideas put forth tonight, and frankly, it is a little difficult to know exactly how to comment, but I would like to take a couple of minutes to go back and really follow a little bit on what Wil Corrigan has said, to provide a little historical perspective for this question, and just review what have been the developments of the relationships between the United States and Japan – in fact, this involves the United States and Europe since the end of World War II. I think it is important

---

[29] "Encroachment of Japanese Firms on Today's Semiconductor and Tomorrow's Electronic and Computer Industries," Dave Packard, 11/16/78. (Courtesy of Agilent Technologies Inc. Archives)

for us to try and look at this problem in the broadest perspective, because what happened last, and what is happening this year, has been indicated by several speakers is really a trend, and not a permanent status of affairs, and I think it is important for us to try and look at the trend.

At the end of World War II, our two principal enemies – Germany and Japan were nearly completely in a state of devastation, and in the wisdom of our leaders at that time we undertook to provide for the rehabilitation of both these countries. This involved a substantial commitment of American resources of dollars and manpower, and it was done with the idea that in order to build a stable world for the future we had to bring these two nations back into the community of nations in a way they would be able to participate with the free world and the future development of our joint venture.

In the cases of both Germany and Japan we invested rather substantial amounts of money to help them rehabilitate their industry, to rebuild their country, and we did this because we felt it would be in the best interests not only of the United States, but of benefit to all of the free world. This process, as you all know, began in the 1940's and continued through the 1950's, and I would like to remind you that during this period the United States was by far the most powerful economic nation in the world. We had a very substantial proportion of the automobile market worldwide, steel production, and almost everything else. Also, during this period the Japanese and the Germans were not allowed to do very much R&D in advanced technology. The Germans, for example, were not allowed to do anything in terms of microwave R&D. I guess the Japanese were about in the same fix, and at about that time our government had undertaken to support a very substantial level of research and development that incurred to the benefit of the electronic industry. This effort was underwritten originally by the Office of Naval Research. They supported some extremely important research and development – some here at Stanford, and other universities around the country that provided a good deal of the basic science and technology for the semiconductor industry, and this of course, included also a number of other areas of scientific importance, materials and energy in others things, but from our standpoint this very important Federal Government Resource of research and development provided a basic foundation of technology that allowed our industry to build and prosper and go, as it has done.

This process continued through the 1950's. We undertook to provide for the defense of Japan at that time, and then moving on into the 1960's we became involved in Viet Nam, and toward the end of that decade we were spending 9.5% of our Gross National Product on defense. Japan was spending less than 1% of her GNP. We were diverting a very substantial part of our resources to the national security of Japan, and what we thought would be the security of the Asian Theater, and of Europe and NATO, etc., and this was a very tremendous burden that Japan and Germany and the other countries did not have. Fortunately, for our industry, the defense effort did, as I have indicated, provide a very important and broad base of research and development that really enabled the electronics industry to make the progress that it made through the 1950's and the 1960's, but it also provided a background from which Japan could begin to build with a substantial degree of partners that has already been indicated between its government and its industry. Now, where we are today, in my view, is that we are at a sort of watershed, a turning point in this process. As a matter of fact, this phase in the relative priorities around the world began in the early 1970's. At that time, as you know, we decided that we had been over-committed from a military standpoint, and we began our withdrawals of our forces from Viet Nam, began to cut our defense budget from what was, as I have indicated, 9.5% of our total GNP, back to the point of around 3% now; still a substantial burden on our economy, and during this period the Japanese were able to concentrate their entire resources toward building up their industry. The effect of this was different in different types of industry – in the case of iron and steel, what it made possible was for the Japanese to have a completely modern facility that was competitive in any sense, whereas we during this period had not devoted resources to rebuild our facilities in the steel industry. In automobiles it is a little hard to say what happened. I would guess I might say that our automobile industry failed to judge the desirability of smaller cars, and probably should have done better. I don't think there was any particular advantage in that, one way or the other, but during this period the Japanese took advantage of their relatively better allocation of economic resources, and also the fact has been indicated that they had a substantial benefit in terms of cost, as their labor costs during the early part of this period were something like 10% of ours, and this really enabled them to move in on some of those areas such as television, semiconductor receivers, etc., with a good deal of success. There is another very important factor in this that has been alluded to, and I think it is indeed an important factor, and that is that prior to World War II the Japanese product had been considered to be somewhat questionable in terms of their quality.

Somehow the Japanese were smart enough to make a very firm commitment to quality after the war, and they undertook to design and develop and manufacture products which would meet the highest quality standards of anywhere in the world, and they tried to deal with the requirements of their customers, as was indicated by one of our previous speakers. The fact that they had very close cooperation between industry and government, the fact that they made a substantial commitment, the fact that they had a very important reason to work hard to rebuild their economy, whereas we were sort of the "top" poking along, and did not have a corresponding commitment – I think all of these factors were conducive to the very impressive development that the Japanese economy has made during the last few decades, whether it be in electronics, semiconductors, or in other aspects of their industry.

In the first place, there is nothing that we can do to go back and change what has happened. This is a development that I think came out of a historical background that had had very good policy reasons as far as the United States is concerned, and one of the, I think, significant factors of our foreign policy during this period is that we did not have any high priority to relate our foreign policy to our own economic well-being. We were looking primarily during this period toward improving the economy of Japan, toward improving the economy of our Western European allies. Our foreign policy was directed at maintaining Japan as an important ally in the Pacific Theater and corresponding priorities in terms of Europe and NATO, and the fact that our government has not been very helpful in the economic field, I think, is in large part due to the fact that there was no particular reason for our government to do so during this period. In terms of foreign policy we simply had things we thought were more important, and, after all, the American free enterprise system was supposed to be self sufficient and self reliant, and not require government assistance. Well, as you know what the facts have been during this whole period, our government has not been very helpful in foreign trade. I look upon the experience of our company, and about 50% of HP business is outside of the United States, I can hardly find a single instance of where an embassy in a foreign country where we do business has been of any assistance to us. In fact, we simply ignore them, most of the time, because they are essentially useless. I think it's understandable; they simply have more important things to do, and after all, the record of American business moving into Europe, and moving around the world was such that it just did not need any government assistance. I think that there is probably an understandable reason for this situation. I think the situation, which we are now facing, as I have indicated, is a period of transition. I don't see that there is any great concern; the statistics you have heard today – tonight, indicate that American industry, the semiconductor industry, is still doing fairly well on a worldwide basis.

I think we now have some things that are moving in a direction that is eminently more favorable. In the first place, the cost of Japanese labor, relative to United States labor, has changed drastically, partly because of a more rapid rate of inflation in Japan, and changes in the international monetary situation. Costs in Japan now, as we measure from our operation there, are now about 10% less than they are in the United States. They are not quite equal, but are approaching that, whereas six or seven years ago it was a very substantial advantage in terms of costs to the U.S.. As a matter of fact, in Germany, our costs are now about 10% higher than the United States, and we can manufacture all the various products here in the U.S. and ship and sell it in Germany or in Europe at a lower cost than we can manufacture in Europe. So the cost factor has indeed become more favorable, and I think this is going to help us not only in the long run, but in the near future. Now, in this regard, the thing that is important for us to realize is that the changes in the monetary system – the changes in the exchange rate – do not reflect immediately in the cost of products. Most of us have to have prices that don't change every day; we have to have prices that are established on a reasonable period of time, and we tend to be a little conservative, which simply says, that we do not, and I think our policies, our procedures are comparable to most other companies – we don't automatically reflect the exchange rate in lower costs the day that the exchange moves; you have to do this over an average period. Now, what's happening as far as our company is concerned, this year our business with Japan, our sales from the U.S. to Japan, have increased very substantially, and it is in large part due to the fact that our products now are less costly in Japan. It is also the result of another thing that I think is important for us to recognize – we have not done a very good job in our selling and marketing efforts in Japan. We are working hard to try to do a better job, and that effort is now paying off, and we are indeed penetrating the market better. We aren't doing as well as we should do by any means, but this indicates that the combination of more favorable environment and a little more effective effort on our part is resulting in improved sales from the U.S. to Japan.

Now, on the other side of the coin, how do we see the semiconductor market? I looked at the figures in our company; two or three years ago we were buying very few semiconductor products in Japan. The trouble is that years ago we started to buy semiconductor products in reasonable amounts. In looking into it, I found that it was not price alone, in some cases not even price, but simply the fact that some of the Japanese suppliers were doing a better job in terms of quality, in terms of customer support, as one of our speakers has already indicated, and this indeed brought us to a very logical conclusion that if we could get better quality and better support, even at a little higher price that might be a better way for us to go. I am happy to report that predictions are that some of our American suppliers have recognized this competition and they're doing a better job – and we predict that our purchases of Japanese semiconductors are going to go down next year, and I think this is tribute to you people in this industry who perhaps responded to competition as you should have done, and simply improved your own performance a bit. Now I guess it was Wil here who suggested that "Buy American" ought to have something to do with this problem, and I would like to say I agree with you. I don't really think there is a great deal the government can do to help us in this situation. There are a few things that I'll mention, but I do think that if we can have a little better cooperation within the industry within the constraints of the anti-trust laws, etc., it seems this is a logical way to go, and a good solution. We have no trouble in telling our purchasing people that, given all the facts involved, we ought to lean a little bit toward buying products from our American supplier, and I would hope that everybody else does likewise. I am not going to define any parameters for this because it depends upon quality and support and price, but I think that there are many cases where we can and should, and our company is giving preference to American suppliers, and I think in a sense we can help to solve our own problems here in this regard, and I would encourage anyone else who is a user of semiconductors to consider this, if you are not already doing this, because I think in the long run it will be to our benefit. Now, what can the government do, and I think the more I delineate a couple of specific things I would like to just put a little emphasis on what Pete McCloskey has said, and I don't want to take any credit he gave me, because a lot of other guys were involved in doing this. I do think we have a great opportunity to improve our communications with our representatives, and Pete has described the problem in very precise and eloquent terms. These fellows have a hell of a lot of things to do; they are interested in doing things that can be helpful to their constituents because, after all, they are not going to be reelected if they don't – and you have quite a bit of leverage here. Even a guy as smart as McCloskey can't know all about all of the problems we have, so I would just like to second what he said. You people who have these problems, just try and think about what a logical solution might be, and give them the ammunition; there have been two or three very good examples in addition to the ones Pete mentioned tonight where this process works, and I want to say I spent a little time in Washington and I know a lot of these fellows personally and despite the general impression, by and large they are very able, dedicated, hard working people. They are trying to do their best for their country and they are very anxious to have help and assistance in doing what will improve the welfare of the country. I think if we would spend a little less time bitching about it, and a little more time trying to help, it would be all to the good, and Pete, I hope we can do this for you. This involves everybody's participation. You would be surprised if you knew how much of an effect communication on the guy back home has. It's fine for a Washington representative to call on one of these fellows, but when they begin to get a lot of letters from the individuals they know back home they've got to receive them, and they've got to take them into consideration, so you've got an opportunity to have a substantial influence here, but it has to be done in a thoughtful, constructive way, and I'm sure that whether they be Republicans or Democrats they will try and respond to things which will help our industry, which will help our community, and if we don't do our job in giving these people some backup we're going to be the ones that lose. Now, as to specifics on this particular program – the problems that we're talking about tonight. There has already been some effort in getting the trade negotiations centered on a more realistic relationship as far as industry is concerned. I don't see that at this time there is any justification whatsoever for differential counts between the U.S. and Japan in terms of products our industry is involved in. In fact, I think we should have found that out long before now. One of the difficulties in these tariff negotiations is that the negotiator has to be involved with the entire spectrum of trade, including agriculture, including all the other industries, as well as our own industry. Agriculture is a very important export in the State of California, and Japan is one of the important customers for our agricultural products, and the negotiators working on these matters have to think a little about the agricultural industry, so there is not the opportunity there to be arbitrary about these matters. There has to be a certain amount of trade-offs, and we have had the opportunity to work very closely with the people filling the trade negotiations, and working on them; and I think, all in all, we are going to come out with a pretty good package, but I think you have to understand that there will be trade-offs at the last minute. You can't expect them to simply look upon our industry as the only industry in the country and come out with exactly what we want, and I think things are moving along very well.

The second thing that I think our government can do really relates to a little of this historical background that I talked about – of the State Department, the Defense Department, and the Treasury Department. I have been looking at our foreign policy in these larger aspects and the impact of foreign policy on trade has not had a very high priority. Recently, there has been a good deal of talk about human rights, and emphasis on human rights, and there is no question but that this emphasis on human rights has resulted in serious damage to our trade, not only with our trade with the Soviet Union and the Iron Curtain Countries, but with countries like Brazil but other countries which traditionally have been good friends. In the case of Brazil, they simply resent our telling them how they should handle their domestic affairs, and they have placed some very substantial orders for electrical equipment with Europe simply because they resent the way our government has handled this human rights matter. This subject is before the Congress – I testified on it a few weeks ago – and I think this is something you people can help with because this indeed has damaged our ability to do business with some of these countries, and it has not, in fact, improved any of the human rights things, which I know no one disagrees with the desirability of encouraging people to improve their recognition of individual freedom and human rights, but it simply won't work. All we do by following these policies is lose business, and there is nothing else that is going to come up. Any extent that you can convey that message to your friends in the Congress, I think, will help get this policy turned around a bit.

As far as Research and Development are concerned I don't think there is a great deal in the way of specific action that our government can take. I see a proposal to increase the write-off for Research and Development – well, hell, nobody who has any sense capitalizes Research and Development, so to increase the write-off won't help you anyway. I see some of these proposals that are being set up for you guys, Pete, as being completely naïve, and I don't really think there is a hell of a lot the government can do to encourage companies to spend more money on Research and Development. I think that unless we're smart enough to know how much we should spend ourselves and not have too many penalties on the matter, that will be helpful.

One of the things that is a very important element in this equation is productivity. During the last three, four, five or six years our government has done everything that they possibly could have done to reduce the productivity of American industry. Indeed, if you want to do something you just work on getting rid of some of these problems we have dealing with OSHA, which you have already alluded to, "Equal Opportunity" and all the other things, and if we could simply take the people and energy and the money spent on these nonsensical things, and put them into Research and Development we'd be way ahead of the Japanese. Now that's something you can do for us. There are some things that I think can be done and might be helpful in other areas. Over the period since World War II there is no question but that the benefits of military Research and Development have been a very important and constructive factor in our industry. The level of military expenditures should not be determined in any sense by that, but rather by what our needs for security may be, but there are some details of the policy, which could be helpful. A few years ago an amendment was put in called "The Managerial Amendment," which prohibited firms, which were doing work for the government from spending any of their Research and Development money available in the contract for projects, which were not directly related to military requirements. Now this is a completely non-productive way of doing things because if you look back upon the fall-out that has come from military Research and Development over the years we have benefited in many ways from things that were done initially for the military, and then it turned out to be useful for civilian use. It seems to me then it would be wise to encourage defense contractors to spend a little time and a little effort thinking about how they could apply the technology they are developing for military weapons in products and applications for peaceful uses. This would generate a fallout and this – is specifically prohibited in the law, and Pete, that's something else, now, that you can work on for us.

We, ladies and gentlemen, we could go on – there are lots of other things – but it seems to me this has been a very worthwhile discussion, and all I can say is that I agree with everything everybody has said here. I really think the solution to this problem is in our own hands, and let's look at the ways that we can solve these problems ourselves. There is one final comment I want to make, and that's in relation to the comments our original speaker made. I think what he said implies a little lack of responsibility, and on thinking about it, he might have been talking to me about the Hewlett Packard Company when he said these things. The supplier relationship is extremely important and in the urgency to meet sales quotas and all these other things, if all of us can think a little more about the other guy, and not place double orders, have a better understanding, better rapport, and communications, I think we're going to improve the quality that's success in the future of the entire industry, and I want you to think very seriously about what our initial speaker said, and all of you guys that are down on the firing line, no matter what your bosses say, let's see if you can do a little better in the future. Thank you very much.

Chapter 15

Business in Silicon Valley

"...It is very difficult to plan a business program in such an environment.
Unless and until I feel that there is a more friendly climate toward business
in the community, I am unwilling to allow any more expansion in Palo
Alto than is absolutely necessary..." [30]

Bill Hewlett

---

[30] "Environment and Social Forces Affecting Business in the Bay Area,"
by Bill Hewlett, 11/30/72. (Courtesy of Agilent Technologies Inc.
Archives)

Environmental and Social Forces Affecting Business In The Bay Area [31]

by
William R. Hewlett

to
Bay Area Outlook Conference
Fairmont Hotel
San Jose, California
(November 30th, 1972)

Environment and social forces are somewhat nebulous terms that could mean most anything. But for the purpose of this discussion, under "environment," I will be referring both to the character of the region in a general sense and to the environment in an ecological sense. I will be using "social forces" in a broad sense to include political focus as well as social.

I can tell you in advance that I feel that the environmental and social forces in the bay area as they affect business are very adverse indeed. Rather than simply develop the negative argument, I would like to conclude with a few comments as to how this adverse climate might be improved. Let me first talk

---

[31] "Environment and Social Forces Affecting Business in the Bay Area," by Bill Hewlett, 11/30/72. (Courtesy of Agilent Technologies Inc. Archives)

about the general characteristics of the Bay Region and their impact on the business climate.

As a city, San Francisco goes back over 120 years. By Western standards, it is, therefore, an old city, and as such it has longstanding traditions and characteristics. It traditionally has been the commercial and industrial center for a large sector of the west. In this capacity, it has built up a complex, multi-racial culture that coupled with its unique location and its generally mild climate, has made it one of the outstandingly attractive regions in the U.S. It is exactly this attractive characteristic that gives this region its "pulling" power, and it is exactly this attractive characteristic that is most threatened by uncontrolled growth and destruction of the environment.

The region over the years has also become a center of great culture and learning. Its museums and art galleries, its symphonies and operas are known throughout the world. It is the home of two great universities that through the years have had a profound influence on the region's development. This influence has been economic to the extent that it has stimulated the growth of the science-based industries of the region. It has been social in terms of the liberal thinking that any great university complex generates.

The region has become the home of some of the nation's largest and most important companies, but at the same time, from a union standpoint, it has become highly organized, as such, it is one of the most expensive regions of the country in which to do business.

Not only has the Bay Area been a leader in business and commerce, but also in many social and environmental respects. Some of these you may be happy about, some you may not.

The Sierra Club, in recent years, has moved from a small regional organization concerned with the outdoors to a major driving factor in the moves to preserve our natural environment.

It is no coincidence that out of the liberal thinking of the region the "Free Speech" movement at U.C. originated and soon spread to the rest of the country. This was manifested by the student unrest that has so marked the last few years of university life.

Out of the desperation of the poverty pockets of the East Bay came the Black Panthers, and I am sorry to say, also the Hell's Angels.

The region was one of the first to rise up in its wrath and say "no more" to the State Division of Highways as it attempted to fill some of the choice sections of the region with snaking strips of concrete.

No, I would not say that the Bay Area is a region without spirit or imagination.

In the strictly environment sense, the Bay Area has latent, if not current, problems. The fact that there are already six regional organizations now operating speaks to this point. Edgar Kaiser will be discussing these organizations and their function later in the morning.

In general, the region has the same problems that many regions throughout the country face – urban sprawl, traffic and transportation, waste disposal, quality of water and air, etc. What makes these problems particularly pressing here is the geographical nature of the area with its narrow strips of land, with its proximity to bay waters, and a natural formation that can and does easily trap smog. But I cannot in honesty say that these problems of the environment at the present moment have an unusually adverse effect on business in the area.

My concern rests more with the social forces that I see acting in the area.

It is always dangerous to single out a single example of a problem. But Berkeley is such an archetype, that in this case, I feel that it might be of value. As most of you know, Berkeley now has a near majority of radical council members. Many of their recent actions might be defined as sharp departure from normal city administration. Certainly one example of this was the initiative measure to set up rent control. As the Chronicle aptly described the nature of Berkeley government, "In much of the business community, the radical presence of City Hall has been viewed as somewhat akin to the Visigoths Sacking Rome."

The latest caper is an initiative measure which, if qualified and passed, would provide that all municipal employees, except department heads and administrative personnel, would be placed on a 30 hour work week, but would be paid a full 40-hour week. There would also be a progressive surcharge on business license rates to finance the additional costs on the added city workers. The measure also would require all businesses employing nine or more persons to establish the abbreviated workweek when they apply for a business license or bid for city contracts. Now this initiative measure may not qualify or pass, but it is indicative of the thinking involved.

Just next door to Berkeley, Bobby Seale recently announced that he was going to run for Mayor of Oakland. He claimed that he was going to "take" the city, with the implication that what is happening in Berkeley could happen in Oakland.

In my own home town of Palo Alto, any suggestion of expansion in the industrial area is met with substantial resistance. At the instigation of the radical organization, Verceremos, the City Council asked the City Attorney whether it could legislate that now defense work could be carried on within the city limits.

It is very difficult to plan a business program in such an environment. Unless and until I feel that there is a more friendly climate toward business in the community, I am unwilling to allow any more expansion in Palo Alto than is absolutely necessary.

I don't want to imply that all communities in this region share the views of Berkeley and Palo Alto, but these views are indicative of the thinking of many that commerce and industry are necessary evils and sometimes not so necessary as evil.

Edgar Kaiser has already reported to you that 43% of the responses to an executive questionnaire indicate that the major disadvantage of doing business in the Bay Area had to do with the high cost of labor and of land; 32% cited high taxes and cost of government; and 27% unions and union dominance.

I think that these factors, coupled with such a negative attitude toward business, has had a most adverse effect on the local business climate. I was recently talking with a representative of a small precision die casting firm in the area, and he reported that of some 60 customers in the Bay Area, 17 had either moved out within the last 10 years or are currently moving out. Of the remainder, ½ to 2/3 are considering such a move. If his firm had not been able to supply these companies after their move, it would now be out of business.

Sometimes it almost seems as if the press conspires to promote these sentiments of disenchantment. If, for example, one reads the press account of the November ABAG report on the need for regional planning and control, I feel one received a very negative view. A careful reading of the report, however, indicated a well thought out and really quite conservative plan.

I think that I have painted enough of a picture to allow you to see why I am concerned about the climate for business in the Bay Region. Let me therefore turn to some possible methods to hopefully reverse some of the trends.

First, I believe that we need more effective and realistic planning – planning that can stand the test of time and provide stability to the region. I realize regional planning may be anathema to many U.S. businessmen, but in operating outside the U.S., one becomes quite accustomed to regional planning, and once you accept it, some of the results can be quite beneficial.

One very important result of regional planning is that hopefully it allows business and industry to make long range plans without the prospect that tomorrow, through some capricious whim of a single community, your plans, and indeed the returns from your investment, can be negated.

The Bay Area has some very special reasons for planning. If indeed the primary asset of the area is its quality of life, then it becomes extremely important to preserve these qualities for without them, we simply become another community. It is interesting to note that 45% of the respondents to the previously mentioned questionnaire cited climate as one of the major advantages of doing business in the Bay Area, and 43% cited quality of the environment, "good area," living conditions.

Business needs planning in the Bay Area – it is going to get it whether it wants it or not, and therefore, it had better get aboard and let its voice be heard in a positive way and not in a negative way.

Secondly, business should bend more than it has been willing to do in the past toward recognizing the wishes of the community. It needs to understand the community's character, its aspirations, its needs and its goals. It is not an easy job as there are many diverse pressures in a community that are not always pointed in the same direction. If I might quote from a speech that Dave Rockefeller made before the American Bar Association:

"As it is, a typical executive may be picketed on Monday by a group denouncing big business for trying to run the country.

"On Tuesday, he may be urged by minority group leaders to take over and operate the public school systems.

"On Wednesday, a delegation of environmentalists may seek to close one of his major plants.

"On Thursday, community representatives may arrive to press for the creation of more jobs and training in the plant's area.

"By Friday, he may speak in understandable desperation to his company's lawyers for help in dealing with Monday, Tuesday, Wednesday, and Thursday."

But there is much that a corporation can do to be a good citizen of a community. Mainly, this is a matter of attitude, an attitude that says, "Yes, this is my home"' rather than one that says, "This is a good piece of real estate with a lot of willing workers and how much can I make from this community?"

But there is more yet that a corporation can and should do. It should encourage its employees, regardless of position in the company or party affiliation, to take an active interest in the community and its political processes. The best antidote for radical thinking is reality. Anyone who makes his living in business – from the janitor to the president – is going to be better qualified to separate fact from fancy than someone who has only a theoretical base for his position.

But not all bending should come from the business community. The environmentalists, too, must be willing to make some compromises. A "stop the world, I want to get off" attitude is going to be self-defeating. The environmentalists will, in the long run, lose more than they can ever gain by such an approach, for society will simply brush them by as unrealistic dreamers.

Let me cite an example of rigid, unrealistic thinking by some environmentalists. A recent Sierra Club report, addressing itself to the question of new power plants in California, states that these plants "take up an inordinate amount of valuable open space." It went on to state that "should utility projections materialize, gigantic atomic generating plants would line the coast at five mile intervals by shortly after the year 2000.

Such statements are simply untrue. Moreover, they are particularly damaging in that they only contribute to the growing power shortage in our state.

Let me cite another example, one closer to home. My company is planning to build a plant in the Santa Rosa area. This is to be a plant for which every careful planning has been devoted to have it complement the natural attractiveness of the region. Yet some conservationists have opposed any such development even though the unemployment rate in Santa Rosa is more than 9%, and many of its young people must go elsewhere if they are to find a meaningful job commensurate with their education.

So the community, too, must be willing to change its attitude toward business.

An industrial plant is a living thing populated by human beings – it should not be relegated to the wastelands – to the most unattractive areas. Its employees spend one-third of their waking hours there, and they are entitled to pleasant and attractive surroundings. Too often industry is simply looked upon as an alternate source of revenue and no more – something for which the community has no real responsibility.

In Palo Alt, 40% of the tax base is from commerce and industry. Yet only 15% of the employees of the Stanford Industrial Park reside in Palo Alto. The combined profit from the sale of utilities to commerce and industry, plus the sales tax derived primarily from the Stanford shopping center, amounts to almost $100 for every man, woman and child living in the city. A former City Manager once commented that he could run the city without any property tax at all, if necessary. Yet industry in Palo Alto is made to feel like a second-class citizen.

But when all is said and done, the ball is on the business side of the court. If there is to be meaningful regional planning, business must get behind it and push. Business must supply the jobs for our unemployed and under-privileged citizens. Business must be willing to try and "sell itself" to the community and become an exemplary corporate citizen. And business, by its actions, must convince the public that the free enterprise system is able to adapt to changing times, and that it is a fundamentally better approach than that provided by socialism.

<u>*Chapter 16*</u>

Going Home

"This amazing progress in America had been built on the cornerstone of individual people applying their talent and directing their energies and capabilities in an environment of freedom – freedom to shape their lives as they see fit." [32]

Dave Packard

---

[32] "Speech to the Pueblo Sertoma Club of Colorado," by Dave Packard, 4/19/63. (Courtesy of Agilent Technologies Inc. Archives)

Speech to the Pueblo Sertoma Club of Colorado [33]

by

Dave Packard

(April 19th, 1963)

I am deeply grateful for this honor and for this opportunity to be at home again in Pueblo. And I feel especially honored that so many of you took time from your lives to be here tonight. I am, of course, pleased that you give me credit for having accomplished something useful during the thirty years since I left home. But as I review the tremendous accomplishments in the world of science, in politics, in economics, in every facet of our society during this time, I honestly feel I have not even been able to keep up with the tide. In giving me this honor I assure you, you give me more credit than I deserve, but I hasten to add I am nevertheless deeply grateful.

This occasion tonight has, of course, caused me to refresh my memories of Pueblo and the years I spent here prior to 1930. I left Pueblo in the fall of that year to go out to Stanford to college and was home for only a few vacations thereafter.

I suppose we are all inclined to remember our senior year in high school. I particularly remember having to work pretty hard at Centennial to keep up in Miss Melchior's Latin class, in History from Miss Anderson, in Mathematics from Mr.

---

[33] "Speech to the Pueblo Sertoma Club of Colorado," by Dave Packard, 4/19/63. (Courtesy of Agilent Technologies Inc. Archives)

Tomlinson, and especially hard in Miss Cunningham's class in senior English. I remember that we did quite well that year at Centennial in football, basketball and track – and I am delighted to see some of my old teammates from those days here tonight, as well as some of my distinguished opponents from Central as well.

Of course some of my fondest memories of Colorado are the hunting and fishing: hunting ducks and rabbits on weekends here around Pueblo, and fishing on the Gunnison, the Rio Grande and in the lakes and streams above Westcliffe.

I also recall, of course, something of the state of world affairs at that time. It was the era of Calvin Coolidge and Herbert Hoover. There was much talk about war debts and other problems generated by World War I. But the feeling was that America was well isolated, both physically and physiologically from the power diplomacy of Europe. We were curious about events in Communist Russia, but these events were too far away to be of much concern. The prevailing opinion of the late 1920's and the early 1930's was that the Monroe Doctrine – combined with the vast expanses of the Atlantic and Pacific oceans were more than adequate to keep America from being seriously entangled in the affairs of Europe – or of Asia, Africa, South America – and the rest of the world just didn't seem to count for much.

In national affairs our greatest concern, of course, was the depression of the Thirties. By 1933 the Gross National Product had dropped to only $60 Billion. In that period, government expenditures – federal, state and local combined – were only about 10% of GNP, and as I recall, the federal expenditures alone were only 2% or 3%.

This year the combined expenditures of government – federal, state and local – will be higher at a dollar level approximately 2 ½ times the total GNP of 30 years ago. Inflation has, however, reduced the dollar to less than half the value it had at that time and so it is more accurate to say that combined government expenditures today are about equal to our total national production 30 years ago.

The influence of science was beginning to have its effect – an effect which was to be accelerated to a tremendous pace in the years that followed. I remember the first broadcast station in Pueblo – it was located just four doors north of us on High Street – in about 1924. By 1930 broadcasting was well established throughout the country, but programs from Europe were not yet feasible. Television had been produced in the laboratory – but much more research was needed to make it practical. The automobile was an important part of our economy – and, of course, of our every-day lives. Air travel was just beginning – but it was more of an experience than a service – and the speed only a bit over 100 miles per hour.

All in all, the future looked bright to me in those days – despite the depression. But looking back, the things which have come about in these past three decades have been more extensive than any of us could have imagined in our wildest dreams.

The rise of Hitler and World War II galvanized the latent strength and capability of our county – and we found ourselves in a position of undisputed world leadership. Following the war, new forces have come to bear to make the world of 1963 totally different from the world of 1931. We understand some of these forces – but we do not yet know how to cope with them. We do not know in what way they will affect the future of our country, nor, for that matter, how they will affect the future of each of us as individuals.

Among the forces which have changed the face of our world in these three decades are the revolution in communication; the revolution in transportation; and the revolution in our knowledge of, and therefore, our ability to master nature and our physical environment.

Radio, television, teletype, the vast array of publications of all types, bring to a majority of the people everywhere in the world considerable information about what is going on everywhere else. New ideas and aspirations are generated. Some come simply from more knowledge; some from advocates of various causes. These changes in attitudes have come about largely because the ability of people to communicate with each other has been vastly increased in the last three decades. These communication capabilities have, in their technical aspect, no ability to discriminate between truth and falsehood. They can transmit bad ideas as well as good, and from all this arises a new concern among millions of people as to whether their lot in life is what it should be. We see signs of this everywhere – conflict – as more people learn that their lot in life can be improved, as the underprivileged see and hear what can be done. These pressures will continue to increase and become more widespread. The revolution in communication we have witnessed may turn out to be a boon for mankind. It may, on the other hand, be a Pandora's Box – and one already opened. In any case, it is a fact and must be dealt with.

The advancement of our skill in transportation is having a similar effect. In 1930, the dimensions of the world were measured in weeks; now they are measured in minutes. In 1932 an American amateur, Frank H. Hawkes, set a new world record for speed – 295 miles per hour. Last year our astronauts traveled 18,000 miles per hour – around the world in 90 minutes. To give you a better idea of just how fast that is, it is a man traveling nearly 10 times the speed of a bullet from a 30-30 carbine. The once vast expanses of the Atlantic and Pacific are "vast" no more. And under the present administration we no long have even the comfort of the Monroe Doctrine.

Whatever way our society decides to use these tremendous advances in communication and transportation, they are only two of the many advances, which have come from our expanding science.

In medicine we have conquered some of the most serious diseases of man and increased life expectancy to over 70 years. But again we find this had raised a serious problem – a population explosion which is going to make it extremely difficult to convert whatever gross gains we make into gains for the individual.

In the last three decades we have increased the generation of electrical energy so as to have six times as much available for our factories and for our homes as we had in 1930. Here, fortunately, we have much more electrical energy available for each individual as well. The development of nuclear energy gives us unlimited support for every conceivable need – limited now only to the economies of the demand.

To give a complete inventory of the tremendous advances which have been achieved since I left Pueblo 30 years ago is beyond the scope of my remarks tonight. I am sure you will agree that what has happened has been considerable in magnitude and scope. And this progress has also generated some problems for us which are of equal magnitude and scope.

The continuation of this progress emanating from science and the solution of the problems which it is generating will tax to the limit the intellectual capabilities of our civilization. These are matters, which will not yield to blind application of force or to action based on emotion. They will, instead, yield only to education.

The education of scientists to carry our technology forward in the future is a matter of great importance. But of even greater importance is the development of leadership which can better understand and meter the great social and human problems, which we are generating with our science. Perhaps we will somehow find solutions through divine guidance – perhaps we can somehow turn the clock back to what many think of as the Good Old Days. It is my view that we can and will find solutions for these problems in the future. It will require more knowledge and more wisdom than we now have – and this can come only from better education at all levels.

We can see how this comes about by looking at some trends close to home.

The economy of Colorado was built on mining, and then agriculture, just as the economy of America as a whole was determined by bountiful natural resources until the first half of the 20th Century. The rapid increase in our knowledge has made a decisive change in our economy, particularly since 1940. Whole new industries have developed, such as the electronic industry, which do not depend at all on natural resources, but rather educated people. At the same time, research and the application of machinery have so increased the efficiency of agriculture and other natural resource industries as to substantially reduce the number of people needed to meet our production requirements. In the past three decades the number of farm workers has decreased by over 50% -- while more foodstuffs have been produced. Colorado produced over $50 million worth of gold and other metals for a number of years prior to 1920.

Mining is an important occupation, but the number of people engaged will continue to decline as more and better machinery and methods are applied to the job. Since 1930, the number of professional people employed in America has doubled, and the trend is upward at a rapid rate.

Our economy in America has changed from one dependent on new material to one primarily on new educated people. The future of Colorado may be enhanced by further mineral discoveries, and water will, of course, play an important role. But far more important is the quality and extent of the educational opportunities you are able to provide for your men and women – old as well as young. New industries will be attracted by the number and quality of your college and university graduates. And they will find ways to establish new ventures as well as strengthen old ones. You already have excellent colleges and universities here in the state. But you must continue to improve them for the benefit of your young people. Educational opportunities are needed, too, for older people whose jobs must change with the changing world.

While I have touched on some of the things that have happened since I left Pueblo, I want to add a comment on why, in my opinion, our country has been at the forefront of this amazing progress. If one examines the progress in every area –

communication, transportation, education, in the discovery and application of new knowledge in every field – it has in every case been motivated by the drive of our private enterprise system. The growth of radio from the old crystal set to the satellite communication system is the story of individual people working in private enterprise. America has more electric power capacity than the new five nations combined – not because of our public power projects, but because of the initiative and capability of our privately owned utilities. Private firms developed the airplane from the beginning to modern jet. Private enterprise has built the finest air transportation system in the world. The American farmer with his eye on his herd, using machinery developed by private enterprise, has made our agriculture the most efficient in the world.

And, not least of all, it has been our great privately supported and, therefore, independent universities which have provided most of the leadership for all of the higher education in America.

This amazing progress in America had been built on the cornerstone of individual people applying their talent and directing their energies and capabilities in an environment of freedom – freedom to shape their lives as they see fit. Nowhere in history has any other social order been so effective in advancing the welfare of its people.

But, as each of you well know, this American way of life of ours has been challenged and is under attack. Krushchev and his

Communists have threatened to "bury us." Socialists in our government – among our people – would place the importance of the state above the importance of the individual. They would direct our lives from Washington. They would take our wealth and distribute it as they see fit.

Colorado was built by resourceful individuals working against many handicaps – individuals who wrestled minerals from the rocks of the mountains – individuals who turned arid plains by irrigation into fertile gardens. This is a tradition, which we must all work to preserve.

The entire prosperity of Colorado, indeed of the entire Western World, will not be generated at the State House in Denver or in the White House in Washington, but rather by resourceful individuals throughout our society – applying their talent and their ability to the myriad of problems, which always stand in the way of progress.

I am profoundly grateful for this opportunity to be here with you tonight. I assure you, too, that such success as has come my way is in no small measure a direct result of the influence of Pueblo – and of the Colorado I remember and cherish.

Appendix A

Dave Packard's 11 simple rules [34]

"Elegant" and "timeless" describe 11 simple rules first presented by Dave Packard at HP's second annual management conference in 1958 in Sonoma, California.

11 simple rules

1. Think first of the other fellow. This is THE foundation -- the first requisite -- for getting along with others. And it is the one truly difficult accomplishment you must make. Gaining this, the rest will be "a breeze."

2. Build up the other person's sense of importance. When we make the other person seem less important, we frustrate one of his deepest urges. Allow him to feel equality or superiority, and we can easily get along with him.

3. Respect the other man's personality rights. Respect as something sacred the other fellow's right to be different from you. No two personalities are ever molded by precisely the same forces.

---

[34] "Dave Packard's 11 Simple Rules," by Dave Packard, 1958. (Courtesy of Agilent Technologies Inc. Archives)

4. Give sincere appreciation. If we think someone has done a thing well, we should never hesitate to let him know it. WARNING: This does not mean promiscuous use of obvious flattery. Flattery with most intelligent people gets exactly the reaction it deserves -- contempt for the egotistical "phony" who stoops to it.

5. Eliminate the negative. Criticism seldom does what its user intends, for it invariably causes resentment. The tiniest bit of disapproval can sometimes cause a resentment, which will rankle -- to your disadvantage -- for years.

6. Avoid openly trying to reform people. Every man knows he is imperfect, but he doesn't want someone else trying to correct his faults. If you want to improve a person, help him to embrace a higher working goal -- a standard, an ideal -- and he will do his own "making over" far more effectively than you can do it for him.

7. Try to understand the other person. How would you react to similar circumstances? When you begin to see the "whys" of him you can't help but get along better with him.

8. Check first impressions. We are especially prone to dislike some people on first sight because of some vague resemblance (of which we are usually unaware) to someone else whom we have had reason to dislike. Follow Abraham Lincoln's famous self-instruction: "I do not like that man; therefore I shall get to know him better."

9. Take care with the little details. Watch your smile, your tone of voice, how you use your eyes, the way you greet people, the use of nicknames and remembering faces, names and dates. Little things add polish to your skill in dealing with people. Constantly, deliberately think of them until they become a natural part of your personality.

10. Develop genuine interest in people. You cannot successfully apply the foregoing suggestions unless you have a sincere desire to like, respect and be helpful to others. Conversely, you cannot build genuine interest in people until you have experienced the pleasure of working with them in an atmosphere characterized by mutual liking and respect.

11. Keep it up. That's all -- just keep it up!

The following is a summary of material provided by the Agilent Technologies Archives.

[1] "Personnel the Heart of Management", Dave Packard 10/8/59

[2] "From the President's Desk," HP Magazine August/ September issue 1973.

[3] "Supervisory Development Program," by Dave Packard, 3/8/60.

[4] "The Humanside of Management," by Bill Hewlett, 3/25/82.

[5] "Technology and Profitable Growth" Bill Hewlett, 4/20/77.

[6] "Managing Hewlett Packard for the Future," by Dave Packard, 3/17/75.

[7] "A Management Code of Ethics," by Dave Packard, 1/24/58.

[8] "Business as a Social Institution," by Dave Packard, 5/6/66.

[9] "Business Management and Social Responsibilities," by Dave Packard, 5/17/65.

[10] "Acceptance Speech for Business Statesman of the Year," by Bill Hewlett, 4/13/70.

[11] "Memo to the employees," by Bill Hewlett, 11/63.

[12] "Inventory Management and Control," by Dave Packard, 11/17/77.

[13] "Tape Transcription of Remarks by President Bill Hewlett, Meeting of Managers and Supervisors," by Bill Hewlett, 7/1/70.

[14] "Making Maximum Utilization of Corporate Resources," by Dave Packard, 9/19/63.

[15] "Encroachment of Japanese Firms on Today's Semiconductor and Tomorrow's Electronic and Computer Industries," by Dave Packard, 11/16/78.

[16] "Environment and Social Forces Affecting Business in the Bay Area," by Bill Hewlett, 11/30/72.

[17] "Speech to the Pueblo Sertoma Club of Colorado," by Dave Packard, 4/19/63.

[18] "Dave Packard's 11 Simple Rules," by Dave Packard, 1958.

Made in the USA
Lexington, KY
05 December 2009